JOHN MILTON'S
THE BOOK OF ELEGIES

Translated by

A. M. Juster

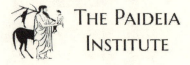
THE PAIDEIA
INSTITUTE

Copyright © 2018 A. M. Juster.

All rights reserved. No part of this book may be reproduced, stored, or transmitted by any means—whether auditory, graphic, mechanical, or electronic—without written permission of both publisher and author, except in the case of brief excerpts used in critical articles and reviews. Unauthorized reproduction of any part of this work is illegal and is punishable by law.

Copyright © 2018 Paideia Institute for Humanistic Study, Inc.

All rights reserved.

First printing, 2018

ISBN: 978-1-7324750-2-1

The Paideia Institute for Humanistic Study, Inc.
www.paideiainstitute.org

The Elegiac John Milton

Few poets intimidate readers more than John Milton (1608-1674). Despite his three marriages, Hollywood would never greenlight a film called *Milton in Love*; we simply do not relate to the forbidding Milton in the way that we relate to Shakespeare.

Paradise Lost dominates our view of the poet. We tend to think of him as a grim, aloof ideologue who inhabited a magnificent but joyless world. Many of his political tracts and mature poems reinforce that image. Most readers find it hard to imagine a witty Milton, an insecure Milton, or a lovesick (even raunchy) Milton. It is even harder to imagine Milton joking about the Trinity as he does in *Elegiarum Liber*.

Trying to understand the young Milton is essential to trying to understand the mature legend. His insistent Latinity in tone, vocabulary, and allusiveness results from his intense early study of classical literature as part of his preparation to be a great poet—in Latin.

Milton's initial choice of poetic language was not as odd as it seems today. Latin had been the common language of European literature for over fifteen hundred years; poets hoping to leave a permanent legacy were still wary of writing in the vernacular. Petrarch, for instance, went to his grave confident that his legacy was his turgid Latin epic *Africa*, not his striking and inventive sonnets in Italian.

As late as the Romantic era, such poets as Walter Savage Landor were still hedging their bets by writing Latin poetry. This tradition ended, perhaps fittingly, with the great poet and classical scholar A.E. Housman, who wrote a romantic yet heartbreaking love elegy for the unrequited love of his life, Moses Jackson.

The young Milton worked hard to master the great works of the classical tradition; he blamed his weak vision on late nights studying those texts. Before long he moved past translating assigned English texts into Latin poetry as an exercise and began writing original Latin verse. Milton matriculated at Cambridge at the age of sixteen, and most scholars date his elegies from his undergraduate years of 1625-1629. His first published poem (perhaps involuntarily published) was *On Shakespeare* in the Second Folio of 1630.

It is difficult to assess the significance of Milton's decision to write a "book" of elegies. In the classical era Gallus, followed by Ovid, Propertius and Tibullus, used elegiac couplets for "love elegies"—generally poems that were much more laments for unrequited love than Shakespearian declarations of love. Soon, however, elegiac couplets became the workhorse form of Latin poets. Even the drearily didactic fifth-century *Commonitorium* of Orientius used elegiac couplets.

By the time Milton wrote his elegies, the term had also taken on its most familiar contemporary sense—a lament for the dead. Note Milton's use of this sense of the term in *Elegy* 2.23-24:

> And let despondent Elegy diffuse sad tones,
>   And let sad dirges sound in all the schools.

Elegies 2 and 3 fit this definition of elegy, although Milton seems diffident, at best, about his task in Elegy 2.

Elegies 1, 4 and 6 play with conventions of the love elegy. They are not love elegies in the conventional Ovidian sense, but intimate epistles to the two men who seem to have been important to Milton: his closest friend Charles Diodati (1609/1610-1638) and his tutor, Thomas Young (c.1587-1655). These poems replace the frustrations that come from emotional distance in Ovid's love elegies with distance of geographical separation. In these three elegies Milton's often borrows from Ovid's poems of exile, his *Tristia*, for tone, trope and language.

Elegies 5 and 7, which I view as the least interesting of the seven, lack clear models in the elegiac tradition. They are both densely allusive and abstract. Elegy 5 is slightly satirical of the pastoral poetry tradition without rising to the cleverness of Horatian satire. Elegy 7 is an impersonal discourse about love that lacks the intimacy and energy of Elegies 1, 4 and 6.

For most lovers of Milton, Elegies 1 and 6 are the most interesting poems of *The Book of Elegies*, and they are the ones most discussed by scholars. Some recent scholars argue that there are homoerotic undertones in Milton's letters and poems to and about Diodati. The closest that Milton veers toward this territory occurs at Elegy 6.7, where he refers to *"noster amor"* (literally "our love"—although Latin literary conventions allows it to be translated as "my love"), which is followed by a punning line-and-a-half that declares that *noster amor* is not restricted by *modulis…arctis* ("strict measures").

Elegy I is Milton at his most Ovidian. He wrote it when he was in exile for an infraction at Cambridge—although scholars do not agree on the details of that infraction or the punishment. A future bishop, his strict yet religiously suspect tutor, William Chappell (1582-1649), may have physically disciplined him for whatever that infraction was. Milton's joy at his separation from Christ's College at Cambridge—whether a suspension or a voluntary departure—is palpable:

> To bear a callous master's threats and other things
>   Repugnant to my nature does not please me.
>
> If this is "exile"—back again with household gods
>   And seeking welcome leisure free of care—
>
> I have not shunned the label, nor protest my lot,
>   And gladly celebrate my exiled state. (1.15-20)

After mulling his own "exile," Milton makes the associational leap to his idol Ovid:

> O how I wish a poet had not borne far worse—
>   That mournful exile in the realm of Tomis—
>
>   (1.21-22)

He even goes so far as to argue (surely with his tongue planted firmly in his cheek) that Ovid would have surpassed Virgil as a poet but for Ovid's exile in Tomis for offenses that scholars still debate (Milton clearly saw a parallel to his own more minor offenses at Cambridge). With these jokey lines Milton implicitly places himself in the long line of Latin poets who knew that they could fool around with love poems in their youth—but also knew that proof of greatness required the epic that Ovid never produced.

Milton moves on from Virgil and Ovid to a discussion of the theatre. Until recently many scholars read this passage as his puritanical dismissal of the theatre based solely on his reading. That reading ignores line 39 ("I...love what I have watched") and the extrinsic evidence of Shakespeare's first published poem, *On Shakespeare*, which was published with Shakespeare's Second Folio in 1630.

Recent scholarship shows that in 1620 Milton's father, a successful London businessman, became a trustee of the Blackfriars Theatre; he might have been the person responsible for the inclusion of his young son's poem in the Second Folio. There is also some evidence that the elder Milton composed one of the anonymous poems included in Shakespeare's First Folio. Despite longstanding academic opinion to the contrary, Milton's early immersion in Elizabethan theatre influenced the dialogues and characterizations of *Paradise Lost* and his other mature poems.

There is an air of loneliness about Milton's description of his theatre-going—there is no mention of it being a social occasion. This same sense of adolescent isolation colors the next passage as he longs for idealized young women. It is only in the two epistles to Diodati where we see evidence of a strong interpersonal connection.

In Elegy VI a slightly older Milton continues playing with the tropes of exile and isolation, this time more playfully as he suffers at home and teases Diodati for frolicking abroad. It is warmer and wittier than any other poem by Milton, but it also contains a hint of Milton's later grimmer persona when, in closing, he tries (mostly jokingly?) to upstage Diodati with claims of piety:

> But if you ask me what I'm doing (if, at least
>   You think it worthwhile knowing what I do),
>
> I celebrate the King of Peace from heaven's seed,
>   And happy eras promised in the Scriptures,
>
> And God's first cries, while stabled under the poor roof,
>   Of He who graces Heaven with his Father,
>
> And the star-spawning sky, and singing throngs above,
>   And gods abruptly shattered in their shrines.
>
> I gave these gifts to Christ, however, for his birthday,
>   Bestowed on me before the dawn's first light.
>
> My sober strains from native pipes await you too;
>   You, to whom I recite, will be my judge. (6.79-90)

Note in line 89 his reference to music, another diversion which Milton had not yet rejected. Milton grew up in a house alive with music; his father wrote at least twenty musical compositions.

What is striking about Milton's other epistolary elegy, Elegy IV, is the extent to which it lacks the warmth and humor of the two elegies to Diodati. Its addressee, the Reverend Thomas Young, was a chaplain in Hamburg and had been one of Milton's tutors before Milton matriculated at Cambridge. Given Milton's traumatic experience with his first Cambridge tutor, we could have forgiven Milton had he been sentimental about Young.

No forgiveness is necessary because Elegy IV adopts a stiffly formal tone and reveals none of the emotions on display in the two elegies to Diodati. It is a text that looks for approval from a mentor in its technique and allusions, first classical then Christian. Particularly in light of the hazards Young faced by being trapped between warring nations, the closing couplet feels perfunctory:

> You should not doubt you'll someday savor better years,
> And you should see once more your hearth at home.
>   (4.125-126)

It is surprising that an epistolary poem of this length tell us so little about the writer and the recipient.

There is a similar bloodless quality to Elegy II, a very brief tribute (of sorts) to Richard Ridding, a Cambridge University administrator who resigned in September of 1626 and died shortly thereafter. The two opening couplets flash a little of Milton's sophomoric wit. The first couplet reminds readers that part of Ridding's job description was rousing drowsy undergraduates—undoubtedly a thankless job. The second couplet is darker and plays off the parallels between Riddings' duties and Death's duties. The rest of the elegy is flawless technically and weaves dense classical allusions into mechanical expressions of grief.

Milton's other elegy for a public figure who died in the fall of 1626, Elegy III, is far more subtle and ambitious than Elegy II. Lancelot Andrewes (1555-1626) was a renowned preacher and the Bishop of Winchester who oversaw much of the translation of the *King James Bible*. He also shared the doctrinally suspect Arminianism of Milton's tutor, William Chappell.

The lines "a vision of bleak ruin loomed/That Libitina caused on British soil" (3.3-4) suggests an allusion to the great fragmentary Old English poem *The Ruin*, although Milton's erudition did not extend to that language. Milton's vision that begins in ruin morphs into a more elaborate and uplifting dream vision—the most intriguing section of *The Book of Elegies*. His mournful address to Andrewes first causes a glittering, sensual and classically tinged image of Heaven:

> There everything was gleaming with a rosy glow
> Like mountain peaks that blush in sun at dawn,
>
> And, as if Iris were revealing her opulence,
> Earth glitters in her multicolored garb.

> The goddess Chloris, loved by gentle Zephyr, decked
>   No Alcinoan gardens with such flowers.
>
> The silver rivers wash spring's fields; sand shimmers more
>   Extravagantly than the Spanish Tagus.
>
> Through scented walls there slips the West Wind's gentle breath,
>   A dewy breath that springs from countless roses.
>
> This home is thought to be like Lucifer the King's
>   In distant regions of the land of Ganges.
>
> As I admire dense shadows by grape-laden vines
>   And glimmering locations everywhere, (3.39-52)

The spirit of Andrewes then bursts into the scene:

> Winchester's bishop—look!—abruptly stands beside me;
>   An astral glow is lighting his bright face. (3.53-54)

Milton's imagery becomes appropriately Christian ("hosts of heaven" and "our Father's Kingdom") until the vision breaks as abruptly as Andrewes' entrance. Like the change from color back to black-and-white at the end of *The Wizard of Oz*, Milton's language briefly reverts to the classical ("Cephalus' mistress") after his dream ends.

   Scholars have studied and debated Elegy III for its historical details, but they have not given it the literary consideration that it merits. Its densely allusive initial vision has roots in a number of classical texts, although it is less clear which authors inspired Milton's subsequent Christian segment of the vision. One should probably start with Dante, then consider Dante's sources, such as Strabo's *Visio Wettini*. It is also fair to ask to what extent Milton's youthful interest in dream visions influenced *Paradise Lost* and other later poems.

Elegies V (on the arrival of spring with erotic undertones) and VII (on love) are largely accomplished exercises on time-tested themes. Perhaps an exception to that characterization occurs during Milton's speech in Elegy VII at lines 27 to 46, which seems to adopt a Horatian self-deprecatory tone reminiscent of certain lines of the two Diodati elegies.

Milton also wrote two groups of epigrams in elegiac couplets; both groups have a passion lacking in the longer elegies. One group of three epigrams reinforces the importance of Italian literature and culture to the young Milton, and reminds us that he wrote five superb sonnets in Italian. In these poems Milton rapturously celebrates his love for the voice (and perhaps more given the lustful desires expressed in the longer elegies) of an Italian opera singer, Leonora Baroni (1611-1670). Milton listened to her in London at least one of her 1638-1639 London concerts.

The other group of five epigrams comments on the failed plot of Guy Fawkes (1570-1606) to blow up Parliament. They seem to be presented in chronological order because the first two, direct addresses to the dead Fawkes, are filled with rage. Once Milton vents that initial anger, they become less personal and more allusive—while still retaining much of their ferocity.

The middle-aged Milton took great pains to publish his elegies—even highlighting them as a separate text within his 1645 *Poemata*. His Latin juvenilia, to a far greater extent than his early English poems, created a problem for him because their subjects and opinions were at odds with Milton's later political, religious and esthetic views. To insulate himself from potential criticism for publishing his earlier work, Milton semi-apologized for *The Book of Elegies* with an untitled epigram that holds his youthful Latin poems at arm's length.

It is remarkable that Milton took the risks of publishing these elegies in a violent and volatile political climate. With his most admired poems not yet written fifteen years after his first publication, Milton undoubtedly felt that his poetic legacy was uncertain, and probably still had doubts about English as an enduring language of literature. For these reasons, he wanted *The Book of Elegies* preserved and read.

A.M. Juster

Translator's Note

My goal was to produce a highly accurate literary translation of Milton's Latin elegies along with notes that would help a typical undergraduate. I have also tried to offer a small amount of more obscure information in order to spark conversations by scholars.

Prose and free verse translations of Milton undervalue an important element of his poetry. While it is impossible to replicate the touch and feel of Milton's cadences, for me it is worthwhile to come as close as possible by rendering his verse into elegiac couplets. I have allowed myself a small number of the traditional metrical substitutions of English formal poetry, and I have allowed myself more elision than I usually use because Milton was quite generous with himself when it came to elision—both in Latin and in English.

Milton's Latin elegies present an irresolvable tension between accuracy and accessibility. His poetry assumed that contemporary and future readers were well-read in the classics, so he often identified mythological figures by learned descriptions that are fathomable today by only a handful of scholars. While I have retained a few descriptions of that type, I have usually substituted the name of the figure or place being described.

As a service to the academic community, I have included facing Latin text from the 1645 *Poemata* and flagged in my notes those instances where the text varies from the 1673 *Poemata*. While I concur with the scholarly consensus that the 1673 edition is superior to the 1645 edition, when it comes to punctuation Milton's eyesight was not good enough to check the text (mine was barely good enough) and thus it should not be considered automatically authoritative. There are a few lines where translation turns on differences in punctuation, and I felt that it was better to provide readers with the differences between the editions so that they can make their own choices. See generally Hale. I have also not engaged in the practice of imposing punctuation on a text in order to bolster my reading of it. I have, however, punctuated my translation in whatever way seemed to me dictated by the text and contemporary conventions.

    I want to acknowledge the value of the data bases of the Packard Humanities Institute and Monumenta.ch. for identifying Milton's allusions. For my textual work Harvard's Houghton Library was graciously responsive to my request to review both of their copies of Milton's 1645 *Poemata*. Aaron Poochigian was a helpful first reader and advisor; my linguist wife, Laura Mali-Astrue, also helped in uncountable ways.

A.M. Juster

Elegiarum Liber
Elegia Prima Ad Carolum Diodatum

Tandem, care, tuae mihi pervenire tabellae,
    Pertulit et voces nuntia charta tuas,

Pertulit occidua Devae Cestrensis ab ora
    Vergivium prono qua petit amne salum.

Multum crede iuvat terras aluisse remotas
    Pectus amans nostri, tamque fidele caput,

Quodque mihi lepidum tellus longinqua sodalem
    Debet, at unde brevi reddere iussa velit.

Me tenet urbs reflua quam Thamesis alluit unda,
    Meque nec invitum patria dulcis habet.   (10)

Iam nec arundiferum mihi cura reviser Camum,
    Nec dudum vetiti me laris angit amor.

Nuda nec arva placent, umbrasque negantia molles;
    Quam male Phoebicolis convenit ille locus!

Nec duri libet usque minas perferre magistri
    Caeteraque ingenio non subeunda meo,

Si sit hoc exilium patrios adiisse penates,
    Et vacuum curis otia grata sequi,

The Book of Elegies
First Elegy: To Charles Diodati

At last your letters came to me, beloved friend;
    The paper brought your news and tones of voice,

Brought them from western banks of Chester's River Dee,
    Which heads out to the Irish Sea downriver.

Trust me, I'm thrilled that far-off lands sustained for me
    A loving heart and such a loyal mind;

Some distant country owes me my good exiled friend,
    But will return him, as prescribed, from there.

Washed by the Thames' tides, London transfixes me,
    And my dear Nation holds me not by force.   (10)

Now I don't care to see the reed-choked Cam again,
    Nor does the home denied of late disturb me.

Its barren fields devoid of gentle shade aren't pleasing;
    That place so poorly suits Apollo-lovers!

To bear a callous master's threats and other things
    Repugnant to my nature is not fun.

If this is "exile"—to have gone to hearth and home
    And seek out welcome leisure free of worries—

Non ego vel profugi nomen sortemve recuso,
    Laetus et exilii conditione furor.   (20)

O utinam vates nunquam graviora tulisset
    Ille Tomitano flebilis exul agro;

Non tunc Ionio quicquam cessisset Homero
    Neve foret victo laus tibi prima Maro.

Tempora nam licet hic placidis dare libera Musis,
    Et totum rapiunt me mea vita libri.

Excipit hinc fessum sinuosi pompa theatri,
    Et vocat ad plausus garrula scena suos.

Seu catus auditur senior, seu prodigus haeres,
    Seu procus, aut posita casside miles adest,   (30)

Sive decennali foecundus lite patronus
    Detonat inculto barbara verba foro,

Saepe vafer gnato succurrit servus amanti,
    Et nasum rigidi fallit ubique Patris;

Saepe novos illic virgo mirata calores
    Quid sit amor nescit, dum quoque nescit, amat.

Sive cruentatum furiosa Tragoedia sceptrum
    Quassat, et effusis crinibus ora rotat;

Et dolet, et specto, iuvat et spectasse dolendo,
    Interdum et lacrimis dulcis amaror inest: (40)

I did not shun the label, nor protest my lot,
    And gladly celebrate my exiled state.   (20)

O how I wish *the* poet had not borne far worse—
    That mournful exile in the realm of Tomis—

Then he would not have yielded to Ionian Homer
    And, vanquished Virgil, you would have top status.

Yes, one can give free time here to the gentle Muses,
    And books, my life, entirely transport me.

Here pomp from rounded stages greets me when I'm tired,
    And repartee provokes its own applause—

Or one can hear a shrewd old man, or some lost heir,
    Or, helmet off, a knight's there, or a suitor,   (30)

Or the rich lawyer with a case a decade long
    Booms foreign jargon to a doltish court.

Often a clever servant helps a son in love
    And sneaks beneath a somber father's nose.

Often a damsel, shocked by such new passions, knows
    Nothing of love, yet loves while knowing nothing.

Or angry Tragedy, with streaming hair, contorts
    Her face and brandishes a bloody staff.

It hurts; I watch and, hurting, love what I have watched,
    And sometimes there's sweet bitterness in tears.   (40)

Seu puer infelix indelibata reliquit
    Gaudia, et abrupto flendus amore cadit,

Seu ferus e tenebris iterat Styga criminis ultor
    Conscia funereo pectora torre movens,

Seu maeret Pelopeia domus, seu nobilis Ili,
    Aut luit incestos aula Creontis avos.

Sed neque sub tecto semper nec in urbe latemus,
    Irrita nec nobis tempora veris eunt.

Nos quoque lucus habet vicina consitus ulmo
    Atque suburbani nobilis umbra loci. (50)

Saepius hic blandas spirantia sidera flammas
    Virgineos videas praeteriisse choros.

Ah quoties dignae stupui miracula formae
    Quae posset senium vel reparare Iovis;

Ah quoties vidi superantia lumina gemmas,
    Atque faces quotquot volvit uterque polus;

Collaque bis vivi Pelopis quae brachia vincant,
    Quaeque fluit puro nectare tincta via,

Et decus eximium frontis, tremulosque capillos,
    Aurea quae fallax retia tendit Amor. (60)

Pellacesque genas, ad quas hyacinthia sordet
    Purpura, te ipse tui floris, Adoni, rubor.

Or a sad boy forsakes unconsummated joys
    And, with love stymied, falls while being mourned,

Or, in the gloom, crime's fierce avenger prowls the Styx
    While moving guilty hearts with his grim torch,

Or noble Ilus, or the House of Pelops, grieves,
    Or Creon's palace purges inbred forebears,

But I don't always hide indoors or in the city,
    Nor is the springtime meaningless for me.

A nearby park with its dense elms and its location
    Outside the city with fine shade attracts me.   (50)

Here you may often see the passing bands of girls,
    Those stars diffusing their seductive beams.

How often, ah, I'm stunned by wonders of fine form
    That could enliven even Jove's old age.

How often, ah, I saw their eyes outshining gems
    And all the heavens circling both poles,

And necks that would surpass the arms of reborn Pelops,
    Each colored by the Way that flows pure milk,

And a uniquely gorgeous face, and flowing hair
    That sly Love uses as a golden net,   (60)

And purple hyacinths that pale by saucy cheeks,
    And even blush, Adonis, from your flower.

Cedite laudatae toties Heroides olim,
    Et quaecunque vagum cepit amica Iovem.

Cedite Achaemeniae turrita fronte puellae,
    Et quot Susa colunt, Memnoniamque Ninon.

Vos etiam Danae fasces submittite Nymphae,
    Et vos Iliacae, Romulaeque nurus;

Nec Pompeianas tarpeia Musa columnas
    Iactet, et Ausoniis plena theatra stolis. (70)

Gloria Virginibus debetur prima Britannis;
    Extera sat tibi sit foemina posse sequi.

Tuque urbs Dardaniis Londinum structa colonis
    Turrigerum late conspicienda caput,

Tu nimium felix intra tua moenia claudis
    Quicquid formosi pendulus orbis habet.

Non tibi tot caelo scintillant astra sereno
    Endymioneae turba ministra deae,

Quot tibi conspicuae formaque auroque puellae
    Per media radiant turba videnda vias. (80)

Creditur huc gemenis venisse invecta columbis
    Alma pharetrigero milite cincta Venus,

Huic Cnidon, et riguas Simoentis flumine valles,
    Huic Paphon, et roseam posthabitura Cypron.

Surrender, heroines, once praised so many times,
    And any girl who tempted fickle Jove!

Surrender, turbaned Persian girls, and you who dwell
    In Susa and in Memnon's Nineveh!

Release your sacred fasces too, you nymphs of Greece,
    And you, the daughters born in Troy and Rome,

Do not let Ovid boast of Pompey's colonnade
    And theaters crowded with Italian gowns!   (70)

The highest honor is reserved for British maidens;
    Let coming next be fine for foreign women.

And London, you constructed by Troy's colonists,
    A high-rise crown observed from far away,

You are too happy as you trap inside your walls
    Such beauty as the pendulous world holds.

Fewer stars shine for you in cloudless sky—a group
    That serves the goddess of Endymion—

Than there are girls with beauty and their gold in view,
    A group seen glittering amid the streets.   (80)

It's thought kind Venus came here—carried by twin doves,
    Surrounded by her quiver-bearing troops,

Disdaining Cnidus, Paphos, and rose-colored Cyprus,
    And valleys washed by the Sinois River,

Ast ego, dum pueri sinit indulgentia caeci,
 Moenia quam subito linquere fausta paro;

Et vitare procul malefidae infamia Circes
 Atria, divini Molyos usus ope.

Stat quoque iuncosas Cami remeare paludes,
 Atque iterum raucae murmur adire Scholae.   (90)

Interea fidi parvum cape munus amici,
 Paucaque in alternos verba coacta modos.

But I, while the blind boy's indulgence lets me, scheme
    To flee abruptly from these lucky walls

And leave behind disgraceful halls of Circe's shame
    While using sacred moly for the task.

Revisiting the Cam's clogged marshes still remains
    Along with joining raucous college chaos.   (90)

Meanwhile, accept this loyal friend's small gift:
    A few words jammed into uneven meters.

Elegia Secunda, In Obitum Praeconis Academici Cantabrigiensis
Anno Aetatis 17

Te, qui conspicuus baculo fulgente solebas
    Palladium toties ore ciere gregem,

Ultima praeconum praeconem te quoque saeva
    Mors rapit, officio nec favet ipsa suo.

Candidiora licet fuerint tibi tempora plumis
    Sub quibus accipimus delituisse Iovem,

O dignus tamen Haemonio iuvenescere succo,
    Dignus in Aesonios vivere posse dies,

Dignus quem Stygiis medica revocaret ab undis
    Arte Coronides, saepe rogante dea.   (10)

Tu si iussus eras acies accire togatas,
    Et celer a Phoebo nuntius ire tuo

Talis in Iliaca stabat Cyllenius aula
    Alipes, aetherea missus ab arce Patris.

Talis et Eurybates ante ora furentis Achillei
    Rettulit Atridae iussa severa ducis.

Second Elegy. On the Death of the Crier of Cambridge University
At Age 17

You, famous for your gleaming mace, who used to rouse
    Athena's flock so often with your voice:

Cruel Death, the crier's final crier, takes you too
    And shows no bias toward his own vocation.

Although your temples may have been more white than plumes
    Beneath which we accept Jove hid himself,

Oh, you deserved to grow young with Thessalian potions,
    Deserved the chance to live to Aeson's age,

Deserved care by Asclepius to call you back
    From Stygian currents, as the goddess urges.   (10)

If ordered to assemble troops in uniform
    And flee your Phoebus as a speedy herald,

You stood just like winged Hermes in Troy's court, dispatched
    From the celestial citadel of Jove,

Like Eurybates bringing Agamemnon's harsh
    Commands to furious Achilles' face.

Magna sepulchorum regina, satelles Averni
    Saeva nimis Musis, Palladi saeva nimis.

Quin illos rapias qui pondus inutile terrae,
    Turba quidem est telis ista petenda tuis.   (20)

Vestibus hunc igitur pullis Academia luge,
    Et madeant lachrymis nigra feretra tuis.

Fundat et ipsa modos querebunda Elegeia tristes,
    Personet et totis naenis moesta scholis.

The servant of Avernus, mighty queen of tombs,
    Too cruel to Muses, to Pallas too cruel,

Why don't you take those who are Earth's useless burdens?
    There is a throng at which to aim your arms.   (20)

So mourn him, Academia, in somber clothes,
    And let the blackened bier be soaked with tears,

And grieving Elegy herself emit sad tones,
    And gloomy dirges echo in all schools.

Elegia Tertia, In Obitum Praesulis Wintoniensis
Anno Aetatis 17

Mosteus eram, et tacitus nullo comitante sedebam,
    Haerebantque animo tristia plura meo,

Protinus en subiit funestae cladis imago
    Fecit in Angliaco quam Libitina solo;

Dum procerum ingressa est splendentes marmore turres
    Dira sepulchrali mors metuenda face;

Pulsavitque auro gravidos et iaspide muros,
    Nec metuit satrapum sternere falce greges.

Tunc memini clarique ducis, fratrisque verendi
    Intempestivis ossa cremata rogis. (10)

Et memini Heroum quos vidit ad aethera raptos,
    Flevit et amissos Belgia tota duces.

At te praecipue luxi, dignissime praesul,
    Wintoniaeque olim gloria magna tuae;

Delicui fletu, et tristi sic ore querebar,
    Mors fera Tartareo diva secunda Iovi,

Third Elegy. On the Death of the Bishop of Winchester
At the Age of 17

I had despaired, and sat in silence all alone,
    And waves of grief were clinging to my soul.

Just then there loomed a vision of polluted ruin
    Caused on English soil by Libitina.

As frightening, cruel Death with her sepulchral torch
    Neared gleaming marble castles of the greats,

Smashed the gold, jasper-laden walls, and did not fear
    To cut down hordes of nobles with her scythe.

I then recalled a famous lord and his great brother
    With their bones burnt on their untimely pyres,   (10)

And heroes who all Belgium watched as they were raised
    To Heaven and lamented as lost leaders,

But most of all I mourned for you, most worthy bishop,
    Once your Winchester's important treasure.

Dissolved in tears, I moaned this way in mournful tones:
    "Fierce Death, the goddess second to Hell's Jove,

Nonne satis quod silva tuas persentiat iras,
    Et quod in herbosos ius tibi detur agros,

Quodque afflata tuo marcescant lilia tabo,
    Et crocus, et pulchrae Cypridi sacra rosa. (20)

Nec sinis ut semper fluvio contermina quercus
    Miretur lapsus praetereuntis aquae?

Et tibi succumbit liquido quae plurima caelo
    Evehitur pennis quamlibet augur avis,

Et quae mille nigris errant animalia silvis,
    Et quod alunt mutum Proteos antra pecus.

Invida, tanta tibi cum sit concessa potestas,
    Quid iuvat humana tingere caede manus?

Nobileque in pectus certas acuisse sagittas,
    Semideamque animam sede fugasse sua? (30)

Talia dum lacrimans alto sub pectore volvo,
    Roscidus occiduis Hesperus exit aquis,

Et Tartessiaco submerserat aequore currum
    Phoebus ab eoo littore mensus iter.

Nec mora, membra cavo posui refovenda cubili,
    Condiderant oculos noxque soporque meos.

Cum mihi visus eram lato spatiarier agro,
    Heu nequit ingenium visa referre meum.

Won't it suffice that forests feel your rage, and you
    Are given sovereignty of grassy fields,

And from your stench the lilies wither like the rose
    (Sacred to lovely Venus) and the crocus?   (20)

Nor do you let the oak beside the river gaze
    Forever at the water passing by,

And any flocking bird, although an omen borne
    By wing through open sky, succumbs to you

Along with countless beasts that roam in gloomy woods
    And silent herds that Protean caves shelter.

Villain, since you've been granted much authority,
    Why are you pleased to stain your hands with murder,

To have honed trusty arrows for a noble breast,
    And to have chased from home a half-god's spirit? (30)

Weeping, I weighed such matters deep within my heart
    As dewy Hesperus left the western waters

And Phoebus, having sailed his route from eastern shores,
    Submerged his chariot in the Atlantic.

I quickly laid my limbs upon an empty bed
    For rest, and night and sleep engulfed my eyes.

As I appeared to wander in a spacious field—
    Alas, my talent can't describe my vision.

Illic punicea radiabant omnia luce,
  Ut matutino cum iuga sole rubent. (40)

Ac veluti cum pandit opes Thaumantia proles,
  Vestitu nituit multicolore solum.

Non dea tam variis ornavit floribus hortos
  Alcinoi, Zephyro Chloris amata levi.

Flumina vernantes lambunt argentea campos,
  Ditior Hesperio flavet arena Tago.

Serpit odoriferas per opes levis aura Favoni,
  Aura sub innumeris humida nata rosis.

Talis in extremis terrae Gangetidis oris
  Luciferi regis fingitur esse domus. (50)

Ipse racemiferis dum densas vitibus umbras
  Et pellucentes miror ubique locos,

Ecce mihi subito praesul Wintonius astat,
  Sidereum nitido fulsit in ore iubar;

Vestis ad auratos defluxit candida talos,
  Infula divinum cinxerat alba caput.

Dumque senex tali incedit venerandus amictu,
  Intremuit laeto florea terra sono.

Agmina gemmatis plaudunt caelestia pennis,
  Pura triumphali personat aethra tuba. (60)

There everything was gleaming with a rosy glow
    Like mountain peaks that blush in sun at dawn   (40)

And, as if Iris were revealing opulence,
    Earth glittered in her multicolored garb.

Slight Zephyr's love, the goddess Chloris, did not deck
    The Alcinoan gardens with such flora.

The silver rivers wash spring's fields; sand shimmers more
    Exquisitely than by Spain's Tagus River.

The West Wind's gentle breath, a dewy breath that springs
    From countless roses, slides through countless buildings.

This home is thought to be like Lucifer the King's
    On distant shores within the Ganges' region.   (50)

As I observe dense shadows near grape-laden vines
    and shining points in space in all directions,

Winchester's bishop—*look!*—abruptly stands by me;
    An astral brilliance shines from his bright face.

Down to his golden ankles spotless clothing flows;
    A glowing miter crowns his holy head,

And as the honored old man strides forth in these clothes,
    Verdant ground trembles with a joyful noise.

The hosts of Heaven are applauding with jeweled wings;
    Pure air resounds with a triumphant trumpet.   (60)

Quisque novum amplexu comitem cantuque salutat,
    Hosque aliquis placido misit ab ore sonos:

Nate veni, et patria felix cape gaudia regni,
    Semper ab hinc duro, nate, labore vaca.

Dixit, et aligerae tetigerunt nablia turmae,
    At mihi cum tenebris aurea pulsa quies.

Flebam turbatos Cephaleia pellice somnos,
    Talia contingant somnia saepe mihi.

With an embrace and song, each greets a newfound friend,
    And with a tranquil look one speaks these words:

"Son, come and choose our Father's Kingdom's joys.
    Now, son, be always free of grinding labor."

He spoke, and choirs on the wing were plucking harps,
    But with night's gloom my golden slumber broke.

I wept for dreams disturbed by Cephalus' lover;
    May such dreams as these confront me often.

Elegia Quarta. Ad Thomam Iunium Praeceptorem Suum, Apud Mercatores Anglicos Hamburgae Agentes Pastoris Munere Fungentem

Anno Aetatis 18

Curre per immensum subito mea littera pontum;
    I, pete Teutonicos laeve per aequor agros,

Segnes rumpe moras, et nil, precor, obstet eunti,
    Et festinantis nil remoretur iter.

Ipse ego Sicanio fraenantem carcere ventos
    Aeolon, et virides sollicitabo Deos,

Caeruleamque suis comitatam Dorida nymphis,
    Ut tibi dent placidam per sua regna viam.

At tu, si poteris, celeres tibi sume iugales,
    Vecta quibus Colchis fugit ab ore viri. (10)

Aut queis Triptolemus Scythicas devenit in oras,
    Gratus Eleusina missus ab urbe puer.

Atque ubi Germanas flavere videbis arenas,
    Ditis ad Hamburgae moenia flecte gradum,

Dicitur occiso quae ducere nomen ab Hama,
    Cimbrica quem fertur clava dedisse neci.

Elegy Four: To His Tutor, Thomas Young, Serving in the Office of Chaplain among the Merchants Working in Hamburg
At the Age of 18

My letter, quickly race across the boundless deep;
    Go, seek out German fields across calm sea.

Stop dull delays, and please let nothing block your progress,
    And, as you rush, let nothing slow your journey.

I will myself exhort Aeolus and green gods
    Who curb the wind in their Sicilian cave,

And sea-blue Doris, with a company of nymphs,
    To grant you easy travel through their realm.

But, if you can, you should procure the speedy team
    With which Medea fled her husband's gaze,   (10)

Or that with which the welcome boy Triptolemus,
    sent from Eleusis, came to Scythian shores.

And when you see the golden sands of Germany,
    Adjust your course toward walls of wealthy Hamburg,

Which took its name, it's said, from Hama's slaying, whom,
    It is alleged, a Danish cudgel killed.

Vivit ibi antiquae clarus pietatis honore
Praesul Christicolas pascere doctus oves;

Ille quidem est animae plusquam pars altera nostrae
Dimidio vitae vivere cogor ego. (20)

Hei mihi quot pelagi, quot montes interiecti
Me faciunt alia parte carere mei!

Charior ille mihi quam tu doctissime Graium
Cliniadi, pronepos qui Telamonis erat.

Quamque Stagirites generoso magnus alumno,
Quem peperit Libyco Chaonis alma Iovi.

Qualis Amyntorides, qualis Philyreius heros
Myrmidonum regi, talis et ille mihi.

Primus ego Aonios illo praeeunte recessus
Lustrabam, et bifidi sacra vireta iugi, (30)

Pieriosque hausi latices, Clioque favente,
Castalio sparsi laeta ter ora mero.

Flammeus at signum ter viderat arietis Aethon,
Induxitque auro lanea terga novo,

Bisque novo terram sparsisti Chlori senilem
Gramine, bisque tuas abstulit Auster opes:

Necdum eius licuit mihi lumina pascere vultu,
Aut linguae dulces aure bibisse sonos.

Someone known for respect of old-time faith resides there,
    A learned curate tending Christian flocks.

Indeed, he's more than half a portion of my soul;
    I am compelled to live just half a life.   (20)

Alas, so many seas, so many blocking peeks
    Are forcing me to miss my other part!

He is more dear to me than were you, Socrates,
    To Telemon's son Alcibiades,

Than Aristotle to his noble pupil, whom
    A kindly Chaon bore to Libyan Jove.

Like Phoenix and his half-divine male heir Chiron
    To the Ant-King, so he is to me.

With him in front, I first surveyed Aonia's
    Wild glades and its cleft mountain's sacred valleys,   (30)

And drained the Pierian springs and splashed glad lips three times
    (With Clio's blessing) with Castalian wine.

But three times fiery Aethon noticed the ram's sign
    And cloaked its woolly back with newfound gold,

And, Chloris, twice you sowed old soil with sprouting grass,
    And south winds twice purloined your handiwork,

And yet my eyes still could not feast upon his face,
    Nor my ears drain his voice's honeyed sounds.

Vade igitur, cursuque Eurum praeverte sonorum,
    Quam sit opus monitis res docet, ipsa vides.   (40)

Invenies dulci cum coniuge forte sedentem,
    Mulcentem gremio pignora chara suo,

Forsitan aut veterum praelarga volumina partum
    Versantem, aut veri biblia sacra Dei.

Caelestive animas saturantem rore tenellas,
    Grande salutiferae religionis opus,

Utque solet, multam sit dicere cura salutem,
    Dicere quam decuit, si modo adesset, herum.

Haec quoque paulum oculos in humum defixa modestos,
    Verba verecundo sis memor ore loqui: (50)

Haec tibi, si teneris vacat inter praelia Musis
    Mittit ab Angliaco littore fida manus.

Accipe sinceram, quamvis sit sera, salutem
    Fiat et hoc ipso gratior illa tibi.

Sera quidem, sed vera fuit, quam casta recepit
    Icaris a lento Penelopeia viro.

Ast ego quid volui manifestum tollere crimen,
    Ipse quod ex omni parte levare nequit.

Arguitur tardus merito, noxamque fatetur,
    Et pudet officium deseruisse suum.   (60)

Go then, and on your way outrun the roar of Eurus;
    Through warnings you yourself observe what's taught. (40)

Perhaps you'll find him cuddling with his sweet wife,
    Caressing darling children on his lap,

Or maybe mulling weighty tomes of ancient Fathers,
    Or Holy Scriptures of the one true God,

Or drenching tender spirits with celestial dew—
    Religion's daunting challenge of salvation.

As usual, take care to say a hearty greeting,
    To say what's owed as if your master loomed.

Recall, too, fixing your shy eyes a bit downward,
    To speak these words with modest eloquence: (50)

"If, between battles, there is time for gentle Muses,
    A true hand sends you this from English shores.

Accept this honest greeting, though it may be late,
    And may you welcome it more for that reason.

Icarius' daughter, chaste Penelope,
    Bought her slow husband's stale, yet still true, tales,

So why have I been wanting to excuse clear guilt,
    Which he himself can't mitigate at all?

He's justly charged with stalling, and admits his guilt,
    And is ashamed of having shirked his duty. (60)

Tu modo da veniam fasso, veniamque roganti;
　　Crimina diminui, quae patuere, solent.

Non ferus in pavidos rictus diducit hiantes,
　　Vulnifico pronos nec rapit ungue leo.

Saepe sarissiferi crudelia pectora Thracis
　　Supplicis ad moestas delicuere preces.

Extensaeque manus avertunt fulminis ictus,
　　Placat et iratos hostia parva Deos.

Iamque diu scripsisse tibi fuit impetus illi,
　　Neve moras ultra ducere passus Amor.　　　　(70)

Nam vaga fama refert, heu nuntia vera malorum!
　　In tibi finitimis bella tumere locis,

Teque tuamque urbem truculento milite cingi,
　　Et iam Saxonicos arma parasse duces.

Te circum late campos populatur Enyo,
　　Et sata carne virum iam cruor arva rigat.

Germanisque suum concessit Thracia Martem,
　　Illuc Odrysios Mars pater egit equos.

Perpetuoque comans iam deflorescit oliva,
　　Fugit et aerisonam Diva perosa tubam,　　　　(80)

Fugit io terris, et iam non ultima virgo
　　Creditur ad superas iusta volasse domos.

With this confession, pardon now the pardon-seeker;
    Crimes that have been revealed are apt to dwindle.

No beast spreads gaping jaws for those who quake, nor does
    A lion seize the prone with deadly claws.

Often spear-bearing Thracians' hardened hearts have softened
    With sad pleading of a suppliant,

The hands that are outstretched deter the lightning bolts,
    And tokens mollify the angry gods.

For a while now he has been moved to write to you,
    And Love has not condoned more long delay.   (70)

Indeed, vague Gossip claims (alas, true harbinger
    Of evils!) that wars rage in nearby places,

And that your town and you are hemmed in by fierce soldiers,
    And Saxon generals now prime their weapons.

Enyo despoils the lowlands far and wide around you,
    And blood now drenches fields sown with men's flesh.

Thrace yielded its own Mars to German troops, and there
    Father Mars rode on his Odrysian steeds.

The ever-verdant olive tree is parching now
    And, loathing blaring horns, Eirene flees.   (80)

Look! She has fled the world, and is not thought the last
    Deserving virgin to have flown to Heaven.

Te tamen interea belli circumsonat horror,
    Vivis et ignoto solus inopsque solo;

Et, tibi quam patria non exhibuere penates
    Sede peregrina quaeris egenus opem.

Patria, dura parens, et saxis saevior albis
    Spumea quae pulsat littoris unda tui,

Siccine te decet innocuos exponere foetus,
    Siccine in externam ferrea cogis humum,   (90)

Et sinis ut terris quaerant alimenta remotis
    Quos tibi prospiciens miserat ipse Deus,

Et qui laeta ferunt de caelo nuntia, quique
    Quae via post cineres ducat ad astra, docent?

Digna quidem Stygiis quae vivas clausa tenebris,
    Aeternaque animae digna perire fame!

Haud aliter vates terrae Thesbitidis olim
    Pressit inassueto devia tesqua pede,

Desertasque Arabum salebras, dum regis Achabi
    Effugit atque tuas, Sidoni dira, manus.   (100)

Talis et horrisono laceratus membra flagello,
    Paulus ab Aemathia pellitur urbe Cilix.

Piscosaeque ipsum Gergessae civis Iesum
    Finibus ingratus iussit abire suis.

Meanwhile, war's horror still surrounds you with its sound,
    And you live poor and lonely on strange soil,

And, needy in a foreign house, you seek support
    Your native home did not provide for you.

Homeland, harsh parent, and more fierce than chalky rocks
    Which your shore's foamy surf keeps battering,

Is *this* how you expose your newborns, is *this* how
    You force them harshly onto foreign soil,   (90)

Then let them try to find support in distant lands—
    Those sent to you by watchful God Himself,

Those who send Heaven's happy message, those who show
    The path that after ashes leads to stars?

Indeed, you're fit to live immersed in hellish gloom
    And perish from the soul's eternal hunger!

It's not unlike the way Elijah pressed on once
    By foot into the unknown, distant wastes

And rugged Arab deserts as he fled your clutches,
    King Ahab, and yours, stubborn Jezebel.   (100)

And so too Paul of Tarsus, when lacerated by
    A cracking whip, was banished from Philippi—

And thankless people of the fishing town Gergessa
    Told even Jesus to avoid their borders.

At tu sume animos, nec spes cadat anxia curis
    Nec tua concutiat decolor ossa metus.

Sis etenim quamvis fulgentibus obsitus armis,
    Deque tuo cuspis nulla cruore bibet. (110)

Namque eris ipse Dei radiante sub aegide tutus.
    Ille tibi custos, et pugil ille tibi;

Ille Sionaeae qui tot sub moenibus arcis
    Assyrios fudit nocte silente viros;

Inque fugam vertit quos in Samaritidas oras
    Misit ab antiquis prisca Damascus agris,

Terruit et densas pavido cum rege cohortes,
    Aere dum vacuo buccina clara sonat,

Cornea pulvereum dum verberat ungula campum,
    Currus arenosam dum quatit actus humum, (120)

Auditurque hinnitus equorum ad bella ruentum,
    Et strepitus ferri, murmuraque alta virum.

Et tu (quod superest miseris) sperare memento,
    Et tua magnanimo pectore vince mala.

Nec dubites quandoque frui melioribus annis,
    Atque iterum patrios posse videre lares.

But you, take heart, and don't let anxious hope succumb
    To worry or pale terror rock your bones.

Indeed, for though the gleaming armaments encroach
    And countless weapons threaten you with death,

Not even weaponry shall pierce your helpless side
    And no lance shall be drinking from your blood,   (110)

Because you will be safe beneath God's own bright shield,
    That of your champion and your guardian,

Who in night's silence routed under Zion's walls
    So many soldiers of Assyria,

And put to flight those whom Damascus cast out from
    Old borders to Samarian domains,

And scared dense mobs, along with their shaken king,
    As piercing trumpets cried in empty air,

And a horned hoof was pounding on the dusty plains,
    And a lashed team was shaking sandy soil,   (120)

And one heard neighing horses rushing into war,
    And iron's clang, and soldiers' throaty roar.

And you, remember what is left the miserable:
    To hope and conquer woes with your great heart.

Don't doubt that you will someday savor better years,
    And you could see once more your hearth at home.

Elegia Quinta. In Adventum Veris
Anno Aetatis 20

In se perpetuo tempus revolubile gyro
    Iam revocat Zephyros vere tepente, novos.

Induiturque brevem tellus reparata iuventam,
    Iamque solute gelu dulce virescit humus.

Fallor? an et nobis redeunt in carmina vires,
    Ingeniumque mihi munere veris adest?

Munere veris adest, iterumque vigescit ab illo
    (Quis putet) atque aliquod iam sibi poscit opus.

Castalis ante oculos, bifidumque cacumen oberrat,
    Et mihi Pyrenen somnia nocte ferunt. (10)

Concitaque arcano fervent mihi pectora motu,
    Et furor, et sonitus me sacer intus agit.

Delius ipse venit, video Peneide lauro
    Implicitos crines, Delis ipse venit.

Iam mihi mens liquidi raptatur in ardua coeli,
    Perque vagas nubes corpore liber eo.

Elegy Five. On the Arrival of Spring
At the Age of Twenty

Still turning in a circle on itself, Time calls
    Again to newborn Zephyrs as spring warms,

And freshened Earth assumes a short-lived youth, and soil
    Is gently sprouting, freed now from its ice.

Am I fooled? Or does vigor come back to my poems,
    And does desire, spring's gift to me, appear?

Spring's gift appears, and thrives again because of it
    (who knew?), and asks some challenge for itself.

Castalia comes before my eyes, and the split peak,
    And dreams in evening bring Pirene to me.   (10)

And my heart fevers with a strange inflamed pulse,
    And sacred sound and frenzy stir in me.

Apollo comes himself; I see Penean laurel
    Twined in his hair. Apollo comes himself.

My mind is taken now to cloudless heights of sky
    And, bodiless, I pass through roving clouds.

Perque umbras, perque antra feror, penetralia vatum,
    Et mihi fana patent interiora Deum.

Intuiturque animus toto quid agatur Olympo,
    Nec fugiunt oculos Tartara caeca meos.   (20)

Quid tam grande sonat distento spiritus ore?
    Quid parit haec rabies, quid sacer iste furor?

Ver mihi, quod dedit ingenium, cantabitur illo;
    Profuerint isto reddita dona modo.

Iam, Philomela, tuos foliis adoperta novellis
    Instituis modulos, dum silet omne nemus.

Urbe ego, tu silva, simul incipiamus utrique,
    Et simul adventum veris uterque canat.

Veris io rediere vices; celebremus honores
    Veris, et hoc subeat Musa perennis opus.   (30)

Iam sol Aethiopas fugiens Tithoniaque arva,
    Flectit ad Arctoas aurea lora plagas.

Est breve noctis iter, brevis est mora noctis opacae
    Horrida cum tenebris exulat illa suis.

Iamque Lycaonius plaustrum caeleste Bootes
    Non longa sequitur fessus ut ante via,

Nunc etiam solitas circum Iovis atria toto
    Excubias agitant sidera rara polo.

I'm borne through caverns, shadows, and the poets' depths,
    And the gods' hidden shrines are clear to me,

And my soul watches all that happens in Olympus,
    And gloomy Tartarus remains in sight. (20)

What great thing does the spirit say with mouth agape?
    What does this zeal, such sacred passion, spawn?

Spring, which inspired me, will be extolled for it;
    In this way gifts repaid will pay a profit.

Now, nightingale, obscured within new foliage,
    Begin your songs while the whole grove is silent.

I in the city, you in woods, let's start together,
    And sing together of spring's arrival.

Hurrah! Spring's turn returns; we praise the rites of spring
    And let a Muse perform her yearly task. (30)

Fleeing Tithonian fields and Ethiopians,
    The sun now turns gold reins toward Arctic regions.

Night's path is short; the darkened night's delay is short.
    Trembling, she is banished with the shadows.

    And tired Boötes of the north no longer now
    Is tracking Heaven's wagon on his trek.

Now only scattered stars in all the sky still keep
    Their former watch above Jove's favored dwellings,

Nam dolus, et caedes, et vis cum nocte recessit,
   Neve giganteum dii timuere scelus. (40)

Forte aliquis scopuli recubans in vertice pastor,
   Roscida cum primo sole rubescit humus,

Hac, ait, hac certe caruisti nocte puella
   Phoebe tua, celeres quae retineret equos.

Laeta suas repetit silvas, pharetramque resumit
   Cynthia, Luciferas ut videt alta rotas.

Et tenues ponens radios gaudere videtur
   Officium fieri tam breve fratris ope.

Desere, Phoebus ait, thalamus Aurora seniles,
   Quid iuvat effoeto procubuisse toro? (50)

Te manet Aeolides viridi venator in herba,
   Surge, tuos ignes altus Hymettus habet.

Flava verecundo dea crimen in ore fatetur,
   Et matutinos ocyus urget equos.

Exuit invisam Tellus rediviva senectam,
   Et cupit amplexus Phoebe subire tuos;

Et cupit, et digna est, quid enim formosius illa,
   Pandit ut omniferos luxuriosa sinus,

Atque Arabum spirat messes, et ab ore venusto
   Mitia cum Paphiis fundit amoma rosis. (60)

Since, as with night, fraud, force and slaughter fade
    And gods don't dread the Giants' treachery.   (40)

Perhaps some shepherd, leaning on a boulder's top,
    When dewy Earth is reddening at dawn,

Says this: "This night you certainly have missed the girl
    Who, Phoebus, would restrain your speedy steeds."

Cynthia, when she sees bright wheels above, retrieves
    Her quiver and comes back happy to her woods,

And, scrapping her faint rays, appears glad that her task,
    Due to her brother's help, has been so brief.

Phoebus declares, "Aurora, leave the old man's chambers.
    Why would you lie upon a worn-out bed?"   (50)

Aeolides, the hunter in green weeds, awaits you.
    Ascend; steep Mount Hymettus holds your passions."

The golden goddess shows guilt in her modest face
    And spurs the morning's steeds to greater speed.

Reborn Earth sheds her hated dotage, and she yearns
    To acquiesce to your embraces, Phoebus,

And yearns, and earns them—who indeed is prettier
    As she reveals her large, all-bearing breasts,

And blows on Arab crops, and her sweet mouth emits
    Mild scents of cardamom with Paphos roses.   (60)

Ecce coronatur sacro frons ardua luco,
    Cingit ut Idaeam pinea turris Opim;

Et vario madidos intexit flore capillos,
    Floribus et visa est posse placere suis.

Floribus effusos ut erat redimita capillos,
    Taenario placuit diva Sicana Deo.

Aspice Phoebus tibi faciles hortantur amores,
    Mellitasque movent flamina verna preces.

Cinnamea Zephyrus leve plaudit odorifer ala,
    Blanditias que tibi ferre videntur aves.   (70)

Nec sine dote tuos temeraria quaerit amores
    Terra, nec optatos poscit egena toros,

Alma salutiferum medicos tibi gramen in usus
    Praebet, et hinc titulos adiuvat ipsa tuos.

Quod si te pretium, si te fulgentia tangunt
    Munera, (muneribus saepe coemptus Amor)

Illa tibi ostentat quascunque sub aequore vasto,
    Et superiniectis montibus abdit opes.

Ah quoties cum tu clivoso fessus Olympo
    In vespertinas praecipitaris aquas,   (80)

Cur te, inquit, cursu languentem Phoebe diurno
    Hesperiis recipit caerula mater aquis?

Look! Her high brow is girded by a sacred grove
    Like a pine spire around Idaean Ops,

And she has woven different flowers in her hair,
    And seems that she could charm with her own flowers.

She wreathed wet, flowing hair with flowers in the way
    Proserpine had pleased the god of Hades.

Look, Phoebus, easy love affairs encourage you
    And winds of spring are bearing honeyed wishes.

A fragrant zephyr flutters wings of cinnamon
    And birds appear to bring you sweet nothings.   (70)

Selfish Earth does not look for love without a dowry,
    Nor does she seek desired beds while poor.

She kindly shows you healthful herbs for healing uses,
    And she herself thus helps your reputation.

Because if compensation, if some gleaming gifts
    Inspire you (Love is often bought with gifts),

She lays in front of you whatever wealth she hides
    Beneath vast oceans and the scattered mountains.

Ah, wearied by Olympian height, how many times
    As you plunged into evening seas she asked,   (80)

"In western seas why does the sea-blue Mother greet
    You as you fade while on your daily route?"

Quid tibi cum Tethy? Quid cum Tartesside lympha,
    Dia quid immundo perluis ora salo?

Frigora Phoebe mea melius captabis in umbra;
    Huc ades, ardentes imbue rore comas.

Mollior egelida veniet tibi somnus in herba,
    Huc ades, et gremio lumina pone meo.

Quaque iaces circum mulcebit lene susurrans
    Aura per humentes corpora fusa rosas.   (90)

Nec me (crede mihi) terrent Semeleia fata,
    Nec Phaetonteo fumidus axis equo;

Cum tu Phoebe tuo sapientius uteris igni,
    Huc ades et gremio lumina pone meo.

Sic Tellus lasciva suos suspirat amores;
    Matris in exemplum caetera turba ruunt.

Nunc etenim toto currit vagus orbe Cupido,
    Languentesque fovet solis ab ignes faces.

Insonuere novis lethalia cornua nervis,
    Triste micant ferro tela corusca novo.   (100)

Iamque vel invictam tentat superasse Dianam,
    Quaeque sedet sacro Vesta pudica foco.

Ipsa senescentem reparat Venus annua formam,
    Atque iterum tepido creditur orta mari.

For you, what are Atlantic waters? What is Tethys?
    Why wash your godly face in unclean sea?

You will do better, Phoebus, cooling in my shade;
    Come here and soak your flaming hair in dew.

On the cold grass a softer sleep will come to you;
    Come here and fix your eyes upon my chest.

And, where you lie down, air that gently wafts will soothe
    Our bodies stretched out on the moistened roses.   (90)

Trust me, I do not dread a smoky chariot
    With Phaethon's steed or Semele's ordeals.

Phoebus, since you are wiser in your use of fire,
    Come here and fix your eyes upon my breast."

So loose Earth sighs about her loves; the mob that's left
    Is rushing with their mother in the lead.

Well-travelled Cupid races now around the world
    And warms his dimming torches with the sunlight.

His lethal bow resounds with its new strings, and flashing   (100)
    Arrows grimly shine with their new iron,

And still he tries to win chaste Vesta, who awaits
    By sacred fire, and the unsurpassed Diana.

Venus herself each year renews her aging beauty
    And is believed reborn in lukewarm sea.

Marmoreas iuvenes clamant Hymenaee per urbes,
    Littus io Hymen, et cava saxa sonant.

Cultior ille venit tunicaque decentior apta,
    Puniceum redolet vestis odora crocum.

Egrediturque frequens ad amoeni gaudia veris
    Virgineos auro cincta puella sinus.   (110)

Votum est cuique suum, votum est tamen omnibus unum,
    Ut sibi quem cupiat det Cytherea virum.

Nunc quoque septena modulantur arundine pastor,
    Et sua quae iungat carmina Phyllis habet.

Navita nocturne placat sua sidera cantu,
    Delphinasque leves ad vada summa vocat.

Iupiter ipse alto cum coniuge ludit Olympo,
    Convocat et famulos ad sua festa Deos.

Nunc etiam Satyri cum scra crepuscula surgunt,
    Pervolitant celeri florea rura choro.   (120)

Silvanusque sua Cyparissi fronde revinctus,
    Semicaperque deus, semideusque caper.

Quaeque sub arboribus Dryades latuere vetustis
    Per iuga, per solos expatiantur agros.

Per sata luxuriat fruticetaque Maenalius Pan,
    Vix Cybele mater, vix tibi tuta Ceres

Young men cry, "*Wedding!*" all throughout their marble cities,
    And caves and shores are echoing, "*Yay, Hymen!*"

He comes well-dressed, more stylish in his tailored tunic;
    His scented clothing reeks of purple crocus.

Often a girl, her virgin bosom bound in gold,
    Advances to the spring's delightful joys.   (110)

Each has her prayer, and yet the prayer's the same for all:
    That Venus give each one the man she wants.

The shepherd also pipes now on his seven reeds
    And Phyllis has her songs she joins with his.

The sailor calms the stars with evening song and calls
    Light-hearted dolphins to the shallows' surface.

Even Jove frolics with his wife on high Olympus
    And summons lesser gods to his own feast.

The satyrs, even now while dusk is mounting, fly
    As a swift chorus over fields in flower,   (120)

And with them, tresses bound with his own cypress leaves,
    The half-goat god, the half-god goat: Silvanus.

All Dryads who had hidden in the ancient trees
    Roam through the mountains and the lonely fields.

Arcadian Pan plays in crops and thickets; Ceres
    Is barely safe, Cybele barely so,

Atque aliquam cupidus praedatur Oreada Faunus,
    Consulit in trepidos dum sibi nympha pedes,

Iamque latet, latitansque cupit male tecta videri,
    Et fugit, et fugiens pervelit ipsa capi.   (130)

Dii quoque non dubitant caelo praeponere silvas,
    Et sua quisque sibi numina lucus habet.

Et sua quisque diu sibi numina lucus habeto,
    Nec vos arborea dii precor ite domo.

Te referant miseris te Iupiter aurea terris
    Saecla! Quid ad nimbus aspera tela redis?

Tu saltem lente rapidos age Phoebe iugales
    Qua potes, et sensim tempora veris eant.

Brumaque productas tarde ferat hispida noctes,
    Ingruat et nostro serior umbra polo.   (140)

And lusty Faunus grabs some Oread just as
    The nymph is trusting her uneasy feet;

She hides now, and loves being seen while covered badly,
    And flees, and wants to be enslaved while fleeing.   (130)

So too, preferring woods to Heaven, gods don't waver,
    And each grove has a godhead for itself.

And may each grove long have a godhead for itself;
    I pray, gods, do not leave your wooded home.

Jove, may a Golden Age return you to sad lands!
    Why go back to the clouds with vicious weapons?

At least, Apollo, drive your speedy team as slowly
    As you can, and let the springtime linger.

Let the harsh winter slowly bring extended nights,
    And let the later shadow take our sky.   (140)

ELEGIA SEXTA. AD CAROLUM DIODATUM RURI COMMORANTEM

Qui cum idibus Decemb. scripsisset, et sua carmina excusari postulasset si solito minus essent bona, quod inter lautitas quibus erat ab amicis exceptus, haud satis felicem operam Musis dare se posse affirmabat, hunc habuit responsum.

Mitto tibi sanam non pleno ventre salutem,
  Qua tu distento forte carere potes.

At tua quid nostrum prolectat Musa camenam,
  Nec sinit optatas posse sequi tenebras?

Carmine scire velis quam te redamemque colamque,
  Crede mihi vix hoc carmine scire queas.

Nam neque noster amor modulis includitur arctis,
  Nec venit ad claudos integer ipse pedes.

Quam bene solemnes epulas, hilaremque Decembrim,
  Festaque coelifugam quae coluere Deum, (10)

Deliciasque refers, hyberni gaudia ruris,
  Haustaque per lepidos Gallica musta focos.

Quid quereris refugam vino dapibusque poesin?
  Carmen amat Bacchum, carmina Bacchus amat.

Elegy Six. To Charles Diodati, Loitering in the Country.

    Who, when he wrote on the Ides of December and asked for his poems to be excused if they were less good than usual because of revelry in which he had been caught up with his friends, keeping him from giving himself enough happy labor for the Muses, received this response:

> My gut not full, I send to you a healthy greeting,
>   Which maybe you will need with yours distended,
>
> Although why does your Muse entice my Muse, and keep
>   Her from pursuing her desired gloom?
>
> You want to know in verse I cherish and respect you;
>   Trust me, you'd hardly know it from this poem.
>
> Indeed, our love is not restricted by strict measures,
>   Nor does it come untouched on its limp feet.
>
> How well you sketch dull food and cheery Christmastime,
>   And feasts that praise a Heaven-fleeing God—   (10)
>
> And luxuries, and winter joys of country winter,
>   And French wine drained near charming fireplaces!
>
> Why whine that verse is alien to wine and banquets?
>   A poem loves Bacchus; Bacchus loves a poem.

Nec puduit Phoebum virides gestasse corymbos,
    Atque hederam lauro praeposuisse suae.

Saepius Aoniis clamavit collibus Euoe
    Mista Thyoneo turba novena choro.

Naso Coralleis mala carmina misit ab agris;
    Non illic epulae non sata vitis erat.   (20)

Quid nisi vina, rosaque racemiferumque Lyaeum
    Cantavit brevibus Teia Musa modis?

Pindaricosque inflat numerous Teumesius Euan,
    Et redolet sumptum pagina quaeque merum.

Dum gravis everso currus crepat axe supinus,
    Et volat Eleo pulvere fuscus eques.

Quadrimoque madens Lyricen Romanus Iaccho
    Dulce canit Glyceran, flavicomamque Chloen.

Iam quoque lauta tibi generoso mensa paratu,
    Mentis alit vires, ingeniumque fovet.   (30)

Massica foecundam despumant pocula venam,
    Fundis et ex ipso condita metra cado.

Addimus his artes, fusumque per intima Phoebum
    Corda; favent uni Bacchus, Apollo, Ceres.

Scilicet haud mirum tam dulcia carmina per te
    Numine composito tres peperisse Deos.

Phoebus was not ashamed to wear green berry clusters
    And to choose ivy over his own laurel.

Often the gang of nine—mixed with Thyone's choir—
    Would cry "*O yeah!*" in hills of Helicon.

Ovid would send bad verses from Corallian fields;
    There were no banquets there; no grape was grown.   (20)

Besides wine, roses and the cluster-crowned Lyaeus,
    What lyrics did the Muse of Teos sing?

Boeotian Bacchus soaked a lot of odes of Pindar,
    And each page reeks of swilled unwatered wine:

While the tipped-over heavy chariot is creaking
    And the dark Elis horseman flies through dust.

Rome's lyricist sings sweetly (drunk on vintage wine)
    Of blonde-haired Chloe and of Glycera,

And now, as well, a sumptuous table with rich treats
    Is feeding reason's power, sparking genius.   (30)

Goblets of Massic burble from a fertile vein,
    And you are pouring poems from that same jug.

To these let's add skills flowing with the soul of Phoebus;
    Bacchus, Apollo, Ceres all concur.

Of course, it is no wonder that three gods, conjoined
    In godhead, make so much sweet verse through you.

Nunc quoque Thressa tibi caelato barbitos auro
    Insonat arguta molliter icta manu;

Auditurque chelys suspensa tapetia circum,
    Virgineos tremula quae regat arte pedes.   (40)

Illa tuas saltem teneant spectacula Musas,
    Et revocent, quantum crapula pellit iners.

Crede mihi dum psallit ebur, comitataque plectrum
    Implet odoratos festa chorea tholos,

Percipies tacitum per pectora serpere Phoebum,
    Quale repentinus permeat ossa calor,

Perque puellares oculos digitumque sonantem
    Irruet in totos lapsa Thalia sinus.

Namque elegia levis multorum cura deorum est,
    Et vocat ad numeros quemlibet illa suos;   (50)

Liber adest elegis, Eratoque, Ceresque, Venusque,
    Et cum purpurea matre tenellus Amor.

Talibus inde licent convivia larga poetis,
    Saepius et veteri commaduisse mero.

At qui bella refert, et adulto sub Iove caelum,
    Heroasque pios, semideosque duces,

Et nunc sancta canit superum consulta deorum,
    Nunc latrata fero regna profunda cane,

Plucked gently by a skillful hand, the Thracian lyre
    With golden inlay plays for you now too,

And, tapestries hung all around, a lyre is heard
    That leads their virgin feet with shaky skill.   (40)

May such displays distract your Muses and recall
    What a little drunken stupor drives away.

Trust me, when ivory plucks and to a lyre's beat
    A festive chorus fills the scented hall,

You will feel Phoebus softly creep into your heart
    As if fast warmth were permeating bones,

And, with her finger-snapping and her girlish eyes,
    Thalia will invade your whole wrecked heart.

Yes, elegy's an easy pastime for most gods
    And summons who it chooses to its numbers;   (50)

Erato, Ceres, Venus, Liber come with it—
    And tender Cupid with his rosy mother.

Great banquets, therefore, are permitted for such poets—
    And often getting drunk on vintage wine—

But he who tells of wars and godlike lords, and martyrs,
    And Heaven in the reign of once-great Jove,

And sings first of divine debates of lofty gods,
    Then the deep realms with their fierce howling dog,

Ille quidem parce Samii pro more magistri
    Vivat, et innocuos praebeat herba cibos; (60)

Stet prope fagineo pellucida lympha catillo,
    Sobriaque e puro pocula fonte bibat.

Additur huic scelerisque vacans, et casta iuventus,
    Et rigidi mores, et sine labe manus.

Qualis veste nitens sacra, et lustralibus undis
    Surgis ad infensos augur iture Deos.

Hoc ritu vixisse ferunt post rapta sagacem
    Lumina Tiresian, Ogygiumque Linon,

Et lare devote profugum Calchanta, senemque
    Orpheon edomitis sola per antra feris; (70)

Sic dapis exiguus, sic rivi potor Homerus
    Dulichium vexit per freta longa virum,

Et per monstrificam Perseiae Phoebados aulam,
    Et vada femineis insidiosa sonis,

Perque tuas rex ime domos, ubi sanguine nigro
    Dicitur umbrarum detinuisse greges.

Diis etenim sacer est vates, divumque sacerdos,
    Spirat et occultum pectus, et ora Iovem.

At tu siquid agam scitabere (si modo saltem
    Esse putas tanti noscere siquid agam) (80)

Let him live stingily, just like Pythagoras,
    And let the plants provide him harmless food.   (60)

Let the clear water stay beside his beechwood bowl,
    And let him drink pure drafts from sober cups.

And, to this, youth is added, free of faults and chaste,
    With its strict morals and untainted hand.

Prophet, aglow with sacred dress and cleansing waters,
    Is this how you rise to hostile gods?

They say that after going blind Ogygian Linus
    And wise Tiresias survived this way,

And Calchas, fugitive from his cursed home, and old man
    Orpheus with tamed beasts in lonely caves.   (70)

Like them, restrained with food, a tippler from the stream,
    Homer conveyed Ulysses through wide oceans,

And through the monster-ridden palace grounds of Circe,
    And the deceptive shoals with female voices,

And through your chambers, Lowest King, where it is said
    That swarms of ghosts have lingered in black blood.

Indeed, to gods a bard is sacred, and the gods' own priest;
    His mouth and hidden heart exhale Jove's spirit.

But if you ask me what I'm doing (if, at least,
    You think it worthwhile knowing what I do),   (80)

Paciferum canimus caelesti semine regem,
    Faustaque sacratis saecula pacta libris,

Vagitumque Dei, et stabulantem pauper tecto
    Qui suprema suo cum patre regna colit.

Stelliparumque polum, modulantesque aethere turmas,
    Et subito elisos ad sua fana Deos.

Dona quidem dedimus Christi natalibus illa;
    Illa sub auroram lux mihi prima tulit.

Te quoque pressa manent patriis meditate cicutis,
    Tu mihi, cui recitem, iudicis instar eris.   (90)

I celebrate the King of Peace from Heaven's seed,
    And happy eras promised in the Scriptures,

And God's first cries, while stabled under the poor roof
    Of He who graces Heaven with his Father,

And the star-spawning sky, and singing throngs above,
    And gods abruptly shattered in their shrines.

I gave these gifts to Christ, however, for his birthday,
    Bestowed on me before the dawn's first light.

My sober strains from native pipes await you too;
    You, to whom I recite, will be my judge.

ELEGIA SEPTIMA
Anno Aetatis Undevigesimo

Nondum blanda tuas leges Amathusia noram,
    Et Paphio vacuum pectus ab igne fuit.

Saepe cupidineas, puerilia tela, sagittas,
    Atque tuum sprevi maxime, numen, Amor.

Tu puer imbelles dixi transfige columbas,
    Conveniunt tenero mollia bella duci.

Aut de passeribus tumidos age, parve, triumphos
    Haec sunt militia digna trophaea tuae.

In genus humanum quid inania dirigis arma?
    Non valet in fortes ista pharetra viros.   (10)

Non tulit hoc Cyprius (neque enim Deus ullus as iras
    Promptior) et duplici iam ferus igne calet.

Ver erat, et summae radians per culmina villae
    Attulerat primam lux tibi Maie diem:

At mihi adhuc refugam quaerebant lumina noctem,
    Nec matutinum sustinuere iubar.

Astat Amor lecto, pictis Amor impiger alis,
    Prodidit astantem mota pharetra Deum:

Elegy Seven
At the age of nineteen

Seductive Venus, I did not yet know your rules
    And my heart was devoid of Paphian fire.

I often scorned those boyish weapons, Cupid's arrows,
    And the divinity, Love, of your nature.

I said, "Boy, shoot down harmless doves; unmanly wars
    Are proper for a youthful general.

Or, pipsqueak, lead your pompous triumphs over sparrows,
    Those are the trophies worthy of your warfare.

Why aim your useless weapons at the human race?
    Your quiver has no force against strong men."   (10)

Love would not take it (and no god's more quick to fits),
    And now he fiercely burns with twice the fire.

It was the springtime and the light that glimmered high
    Above the farmhouse brought you May the first,

Though up to then my eyes were seeking fleeing night
    And would not bear the morning's radiance.

Love stayed bedside, a restless Love with colored wings;
    A moving quiver showed a god was there,

Prodidit et facies, et dulce minantis ocelli,
    Et quicquid puero dignum et Amore fuit. (20)

Talis in aeterno iuvenis Sigeius Olympo
    Miscet amatori pocula plena Iovi;

Aut qui formosas pellexit ad oscula nymphas
    Thiodamantaeus naiade rapyus Hylas;

Addideratque iras, sed et has decuisse putares,
    Addideratque truces, nec sine felle minas.

Et miser exemplo sapuisses tutius, inquit,
    Nunc mea quid possit dextera testis eris.

Inter et expertos vires numerabere nostras,
    Et faciam per tua damna fidem. (30)

Ipse ego si nescis strato Pythone superbum
    Edomui Phoebum, cessit et ille mihi;

Et quoties meminit Peneidos, ipse fatetur
    Certius et gravius tela nocere mea.

Me nequit adductum curvare peritius arcum,
    Qui post terga solet vincere Parthus eques.

Cydoniusque mihi cedit venator, et ille
    Inscius uxori qui necis author erat.

Est etiam nobis ingens quoque victus Orion,
    Herculeaeque manus, Herculeusque comes. (40)

And his face showed it, and his sweetly daunting eyes,
    And each thing fitting for a boy and Love.   (20)

He was like Ganymede, who, for his lover Jove,
    Prepares full goblets in eternal Heaven,

Or Hylas, Theodamas' son, kidnapped by
    A Naiad, who lured gorgeous nymphs for kisses,

But added fits (you'd even think these suited him),
    And added nasty warnings—not without bile,

And said, "Wretch, it was safer learning from example.
    Now you will see what my right hand can do.

You will be counted with all those who knew my strength,
    And through your pains I truly will persuade.   (30)

I tamed the haughty Phoebus; if you do not know,
    With Python slain, he acquiesced to *me*,

And when he thinks of Daphne, he himself admits
    My arrows wound more surely and more gravely.

A Persian horseman, brought to kill behind his back,
    Can't bend taut bows more skillfully than *I*.

The man who caused, unknowingly, his own wife's death—
    And Cephalus, both acquiesce to *me*,

And also even huge Orion lost to *me*—
    And Hercules' hands and Hercules' friend.   (40)

Iupiter ipse licet sua fulmina torqueat in me,
    Haerebunt lateri spicula nostra Iovis.

Caetera quae dubitas melius mea tela docebunt,
    Et tua non leviter corda petenda mihi.

Nec te stulte tuae poterunt defendere Musae
    Nec tibi Phoebaeus porriget anguis opem.

Dixit, et aurato quatiens mucrone sagittam,
    Evolat in tepidos Cypridos ille sinus.

At mihi risuro tonuit ferus ore minaci,
    Et mihi de puero non metus ullus erat.   (50)

Et modo qua nostri spatiantur in urbe Quirites
    Et modo villarum proxima rura placent.

Turba frequens, facieque simillima turba dearum,
    Splendida per medias itque reditque vias.

Auctaque luce dies gemino fulgore coruscat,
    Fallor? An et radios hinc quoque Phoebus habet.

Haec ego non fugi spectacula grata severus,
    Impetus et quo me fert iuvenilis, agor.

Lumina luminibus male providus obvia misi,
    Neve oculos potui continuisse meos.   (60)

Unam forte aliis supereminuisse notabam,
    Principium nostri lux erat illa mali.

Let Jupiter himself fling thunderbolts at *me*;
    My arrows will be sticking in Jove's side.

My darts will better clarify remaining doubts,
    And *I* won't lightly take aim at your heart.

Your Muses, fool, will not be able to protect you,
    Nor will the snake of Phoebus offer help."

He spoke, and brandishing an arrow tipped with gold,
    He flew away to Venus' warm lap,

But when he thundered savagely at me, I laughed,
    And wasn't frightened by the boy at all,   (50)

And lately neighbors are delighted strolling in
    The city, then in nearby country towns.

Dense mobs, each face like one from goddess mobs,
    Arrive and leave in splendor through main streets.

With light increased, day doubly shimmers. Am I tricked?
    Or from them, too, does Phoebus shine his beams?

I did not grimly flee this welcome spectacle
    And I was led where youthful impulse took me.

Predicting badly, I cast my gaze to meet their gaze
    And I could not have joined my eyes with theirs.   (60)

By chance I noticed one who outshone all the rest;
    That brilliance was the start of my misfortunes.

Sic Venus optaret mortalibus ipsa videri,
    Sic regina Deum conspicienda fuit.

Hanc memor obiecit nobis malus ille Cupido,
    Solus et hos nobis texuit ante dolos.

Nec procul ipse vafer latuit, multaeque sagittae,
    Et facis a tergo grande pependit onus.

Nec mora; nunc ciliis haesit, nunc virginis ori,
    Insilit hinc labiis, insidet inde genis: (70)

Et quascunque agilis partes iaculator oberrat,
    Hei mihi, mille locis pectus inerme ferit.

Protinus insoliti subierunt corda furores,
    Uror amans intus, flammaque totus eram.

Interea misero quae iam mihi sola placebat
    Ablata est, oculis non reditura meis.

Ast ego progredior tacite querebundus, et excors,
    Et dubius volui saepe referre pedem.

Findor, et haec remanet, sequitur pars latera votum;
    Raptaque tam subito gaudia flere iuvat.   (80)

Sic dolet amissum proles Iunonia coelum,
    Inter Lemniacos praeciptata focos.

Talis et abreptum solem respexit, ad orcum
    Vectus ab attonitis Amphiaraus equis.

Venus might have aspired to look this way to mortals;
    The queen of gods must have appeared this way.

That grudging, evil Cupid pushed her in my path,
    And all alone devised these snares before me.

The trickster hid himself nearby, and loads of torches
    And many arrows hung upon his back.

He promptly clung to eyelids first, then the girl's mouth;
    From there he jumps to lips, then rests on cheeks,   (70)

And on those parts where this quick archer flits (*Oh my!*),
    He strikes my unarmed chest in countless places.

Strange urges suddenly had slipped into my heart;
    In love, I burned inside and was all passion.

Meanwhile she, the sole one to please me in my gloom,
    Was taken from my sight, not to return,

But I moved forward, softly wailing in a daze,
    And often wanted to retrace my steps.

I'm torn, and one part stays; another follows hope,
    And it is good to weep for joys found quickly.   (80)

Because he squandered Heaven, Vulcan mourned like this
    When he was dropped among the Lemnean homes.

And so too Amphiaraus, hauled by mad steeds
    To Hades, looked back at sunlight lost.

Quid faciam infelix, et luctu victus, amores
    Nec licet inceptos ponere, neve sequi.

O utinam spectare semel mihi detur amatos
    Vultus, et coram tristia verba loqui;

Forsitan et duro non est adamante creata,
    Forte nec ad nostras surdeat illa preces.   (90)

Crede mihi nullus sic infeliciter arsit,
    Ponar in exemplo primus et unus ego.

Parce precor teneri cum sis Deus ales amoris,
    Pungent officio nec tua facta tuo.

Iam tuus o certe est mihi formidabilis arcus,
    Nate dea, iaculis nec minus igne potens:

Et tua fumabunt nostris altaria donis,
    Solus et in superis tu mihi summus eris.

Deme meos tandem, verum nec deme furors,
    Nescio cur, miser est suaviter omnis amans: (100)

Tu modo da facilis, posthaec mea siqua futura est,
    Cuspis amaturos figat ut una duos.

Unhappy and undone by grief, what shall I do?
    I cannot chase or give up love just started.

If only I could see her lovely face just once
    And speak my mournful message openly!

And possibly she is not made of cruel adamant,
    And maybe won't be deaf to my appeals. (90)

Trust me, no one has burned up so unhappily;
    I'll be declared the first and best example.

Please spare me, for you are winged god of tender love;
    Don't let your actions war against your duty.

Your bow now surely frightens me, O son of Venus,
    Endowed with arrows and no less with fire,

And with my offering your altars will be smoking,
    And only you will be my highest god.

Banish, at last, my longings—truly, do not end them.
    Why, I don't know—each lover is sweetly sad. (100)

Just kindly grant, if any maiden shall be mine,
    That one sharp point shall pierce a pair in love.

Haec Ego Mente...

Haec ego mente olim laeva, studioque supino
  Nequitiae posui vana trophaea meae.

Scilicet abreptum sic me malus impulit error,
  Indocilisque aetas prava magistra fuit.

Donec Socraticos umbrosa Academia rivos
  Praebuit, admissum dedocuitque iugum.

Protinus extinctis ex illo tempore flammis,
  Cincta rigent multo pectora nostra gelu.

Unde suis frigus metuit puer ipse sagittis,
  Et Diomedeam vim timet ipsa Venus.

[Untitled Postscript]

From a perverse persistence and contrariness,
    I once made pointless trophies to my vileness.

Of course, poor judgment drove me while misled this way,
    And my flawed teacher was my untaught youth

Until a shaded school supplied Socratic streams
    And I unlearned the yoke I had accepted.

With fires doused continuously from then on,
    My heart has stiffened, packed in by thick ice,

So even Cupid with his arrows fears the cold
    And Venus dreads the strength of Diomedes.

In Proditionem Bombardicam

Cum simul in regem nuper satrapasque Britannos
 Ausus es in infandum perfide Fauxe nefas,

Fallor? An et mitis voluisti ex parte videri,
 Et pensare mala cum pietate scelus?

Scilicet hos alti missurus ad atria caeli,
 Sulphereo curru flammivolisque rotis.

Qualiter ille feris caput inviolabile Parcis
 Liquit Iordanios turbine raptus agros.

On the Gunpowder Plot

When, traitorous Fawkes, you dared of late a monstrous wrong
    Against the King, and English lords as well,

Am I deceived, or did you wish to seem half-kind
    And mitigate the crimes with phony faith?

It would have been hurtled them to Heaven's lofty halls
    By sulfured chariot with flaming wheels,

Like one whose head, untouchable by savage Fates,
    Fled fields of Jordan raptured in a whirlwind.

In Eandem I

Siccine tentasti caelo donasse Iacobum
    Quae septemgemino Belua monte lates?

Ni meliora tuum poterit dare munera numen,
    Parce precor donis insidiosa tuis.

Ille quidem sine te consortia serus adivit
    Astra, nec inferni pulveris usus ope.

Sic potius foedos in caelum pelle cucullos,
    Et quot habet brutos Roma profana deos,

Namque hac aut alia nisi quemque adiuveris arte,
    Crede mihi caeli vix bene scandet iter. (10)

Another on the Same (I)

Isn't it true, you Beast who prowls the seven hills,
    That you attempted giving James to Heaven?

Unless your God can offer better offerings,
    I ask you, traitor, spare us from your gifts.

He left without you recently for fellow stars,
    Indeed, unaided by your hellish powder.

So blow to Heaven the disgusting cowls instead—
    And all the senseless gods profane Rome has,

And yes, if you don't help by this or other means,
    Believe me, barely one will go to Heaven.

In Eandem II

Purgatorem animae derisit iacobus ignem,
　　Et sine quo superum non adeunda domus.

Frenduit hoc trina monstrum Latiale corona
　　Movit et horrificum cornua dena minax.

Et nec inultus ait temnes mea sacra Britanne,
　　Supplicium spreta relligione dabis.

Et si stelligeras unquam penetraveris arces,
　　Non nisi per flammas triste patebit iter.

O quam funesto cecinisti proxima vero,
　　Verbaque ponderibus vix caritura suis!

Nam prope Tartareo sublime rotatus ab igni
　　Ibat ad aetheras umbra perusta plagas.　　　　　(10)

Another on the Same (II)

James mocked the purgatorial fire of the soul,
    Without which no one nears our house on high.

The thrice-crowned Roman monster gnashed his teeth at this;
    Threatening and gross, he shook ten horns and said,

"Englishman, you won't mock the sacred unavenged;
    You'll pay the price for having spurned religion

And you will only reach the starry citadels
    If fire opens up a bitter path."

O you predicted close to the depressing truth,
    And with words almost lacking their own weight!   (10)

Indeed, he nearly rose, circled by hellish fire,
    To lofty regions as an ashen ghost.

In Eandem III

Quem modo Roma suis devoverat impia diris,
    Et Styge damnarat Taenarioque sinu,

Hunc vice mutata iam tollere gestit ad astra,
    Et cupit ad superos evehere usque Deos.

Another on the Same (III)

As for the one who faithless Rome condemned with curses
    And damned to Styx and the Taenarian harbor,

She strains now, with things changed, to lift him to the stars
    And keeps on hoisting him to gods on high.

In Inventorem Bombardae

Iapetionidem laudavit caeca vetustas,
    Qui tulit aetheream solis ab axe facem;

At mihi maior erit, qui lurida creditor arma,
    Et trifidum fulmen surripuisse Iovi.

On the Inventor of Gunpowder

Blind legend praised Prometheus, who stole
From the sun's chariot a solar torch,

Though someone thought to have purloined Jove's tri-forked bolts
And ghastly weapons will, for me, be greater.

Ad Leonoram Romae Canentem

Angelus unicuique suus (sic credite gentes)
    Obrigit aethereis ales ab ordinibus.

Quid mirum, Leonora tibi si Gloria maior?
    Nam tua praesentem vox sonat ipsa Deum.

Aut Deus, aut vacui certe mens tertia coeli
    Per tua secreto guttura serpit agens;

Serpit agens, facilisque docet mortalia corda
    Sensim immortali assuscere posse sono.

Quod si cuncta quidem Deus est, per cunctaque fusus,
    In te una loquitur, caetera mutus habet. (10)

To Leonora Singing in Rome

An unsurpassed winged angel (people, trust it's so)
    Is gracing each of us from Heaven's ranks.

Why wonder, Leonora, if your glory's greater?
    Indeed, your tone resounds with God's own presence.

If not God, surely a third mind from empty sky
    Glides touchingly in secret through your throat—

Glides touchingly, and teaches mortal hearts with ease
    To acclimate to your immortal sound.

For if God is indeed all things, and fused with all,
    He speaks in you alone; He stills the rest.

Ad Eandem I

Altera Torquatum cepit Leonora Poetam,
    Cuius ab insano cessit amore furens.

Ah miser ille tuo quanto felicius aevo
    Perditus, et propter te Leonora foret!

Et te Pieria sensisset voce canentem
    Aurea maternae fila movere lyrae,

Quamvis Dircaeo torsisset lumina Pentheo
    Saevior, aut totus desipuisset iners.

Tu tamen errantes caeca vertigine sensus
    Voce eadem poteras composuisse tua;   (10)

Et poteras aegro spirans sub corde quietem
    Flexanimo cantu restituisse sibi.

To the Same Person (I)

Another Leonora chose the poet Tasso,
    Who died while raging from compulsive love.

Ah, wretch, how much more happily he would have died
    Back then and, Leonora, due to you!

And he'd have heard you, singing with your Muse's voice,
    Excite gold strings upon your mother's lyre,

Though, fiercer than Pentheus of Thebes, he would
    Have rolled his eyes or acted mad or numb.

Besides, you could have calmed his senses with your voice
    As they meandered through blind dizziness,   (10)

And, breathing quiet into his dejected heart,
    You could have healed him with mind-bending music.

Ad Eandem II

Credula quid liquidam Sirena Neapoli iactas,
 Claraque Parthenopes fana Acheloiados,

Littoreamque tua defunctam naiada ripa
 Corpora Chalcidio sacra dedisse rogo?

Illa quidem vivitque, et amoena Tibridis unda
 Mutavit rauci murmura Pausilipi.

Illic Romulidum studiis ornata secundis,
 Atque homines cantu detinet atque Deos.

To the Same Person (II)

Why tout, duped Naples, the famed shrine of clear-voiced Siren
    Parthenope, the child of Achelous,

A coastal Naiad, dead upon your shores, who left
    Her sacred body to a Naples pyre?

She certainly survives, and traded sounds of loud
    Posilipo for the Tiber's pleasant waters.

There, honored by the zeal of sons of Romulus,
    She is entrancing men and gods with song.

Notes

1.Title   Charles Diodati (1609-1638) was Milton's closest friend.

1.1   *Tabellae* were wax tablets framed in wood used for, among other purposes, correspondence between friends. Cf. Ovid *Metamorphoses* 9.522; Catullus 50.2; see generally Meyer, "Wooden Wit: *Tabellae* in Latin poetry" in Tylawski & Weiss at 201-212. Milton is being humorous here; he and Diodati corresponded by letter, not wax tablets. See generally Brown, "John Milton and Charles Diodati: Reading the Textual Exchanges of Friends" Vol. 45 No. 2 *Milton Quarterly* (2011) at 73-94.

1.2   The nouns *nuntia* ("messenger") and *charta* ("paper") could be in several cases, which makes a definitive literal translation impossible.

1.3   The River Dee forms part of the border between Wales and England. It had mystical associations for British poets, as reflected in Milton's *Lycidas* 55 ("Not yet where Deva spreads her wisard stream") and *At a Vacation Exercise* 98 ("the ancient hallowed Dee").

1.4   Masson at 299 suggests that the phrase *Vergivium…salum* ("Irish Sea") came from the highly popular *Britannia* of William Camden (1551-1623) and originated with the *Polyolbion* of Drayton.

For *prono...amne* ("downstream"), cf. Tacitus *Historiae* 5.22 (*prono amne*). For a gratuitously vicious, but useful, article on Milton's Latin sources, see Fletcher, "Milton's Latin Poems" Vol. 37 No. 4 *Modern Philology* (1940); see also Godolphin, "Notes on the Technique of Milton's Latin Elegies" *id.* at 351-356.

1.5 Bush notes that *terras...remotas* ("remote lands") probably echoes Lucan *Bellum civile* 774-775.

1.6 Fletcher notes the parallel to Propertius 2.1.36 (*fidele caput*).

1.7-8 For the debt trope, MacKellar notes Horace *Carmina* 1.3.5-8.

1.9 I have rendered *reflua...unda* (literally "retreating waves") as "tides." Bush cites likely sources from Ovid and Buchanan. Bush, Shaw & Giamatti at 48. Today North Sea tides affect the Thames into London. Before construction of Teddington Lock, tides affected the river farther upstream.

Milton is using *urbs* (literally "the city") in the way that Romans used the word to refer to Rome.

1.10 The wry phrase *nec invitum* ("not by force"—literally closer to "not unwillingly") is an example of the rhetorical technique known as *litotes*, a double negative. Use of this device may reflect some arrogance or whimsy.

In English Milton typically capitalized "Nation."

In the 1645 edition the punctuation mark at the end of the couplet is unclear, but context argues for a period.

1.11   The adjective *arundiferum* ("reed-choked"—literally "reed-carrying") is a later version of the rare classical *harundiferum*. Milton almost certainly found it in Ovid *Fasti* 5.637 (*harundiferum*). Students at Cambridge amuse themselves today punting on this shallow, narrow river.

1.12   The primary meaning of *laris* was the Lares, minor gods of the household. The term became a metonym for "hearth" and "home."

Scholars debate whether *dudum vetiti* ("forbidden lately") refers to a suspension from Cambridge for arguing with his tutor (my view in light of line 15) or to a vacation. The phrase could also mean "recently rejected." See generally Bush, Shaw & Giamatti at 44-46.

1.13   Revard (1997) notes at 14 that the phrase *molles...umbras* ("gentle shade") probably echoes Propertius 3.3.1 or Catullus 66.55. The 1645 edition appears to be *molle*, but that is clearly a typographical error.

1.14   The term *Phoebicolis* ("Apollo-lovers") refers to poets. Phoebus, also known as Apollo, was the god of poetry. Bush notes that Scaliger was the likely coiner of this word. See Bush, Shaw & Giamatti at 49.

I have translated this line as "That place so badly...." rather than "How badly that place..." to give the line the force it has in Latin.

The punctuation mark at the end of the line is unclear in the 1645 edition, but is almost surely a period.

1.16 There is disputed lore that Milton's tutor, William Chappell, whipped him for some offense. The offense need not have been committed in the classroom because Chappel and Milton also shared living quarters, a standard arrangement in that day.

The 1645 edition has a comma at the end of the line, but that is almost surely a typographical error.

1.17 The Penates were household gods similar to the Lares. Cf. n.1.12 *supra*.

In this line *hoc* ("this") appears to be treated as a short syllable, which raises a metrical issue.

I believe *adiisses* is a typographical error and have emended it to *adiisse* ("to have gone"), which is the only way the line makes sense.

1.18 For possible sources of *vacuum curis* ("free of worries") and *otia grata* ("welcome pastimes"), see Bush, Shaw & Giamatti at 49.

1.19 The phrase *profugi nomen* ("I have…shunned the label") echoes Ovid *Tristia* 5.406 (*profugi nomen*).

1.21 Milton's *vates* ("the bard") refers to Ovid. For more on Milton's early study of Ovid, see DuRocher at 38-47; see generally Kilgour. For a useful article arguing that Milton's Latin prosody relies more on Ovid than Virgil, see Duckworth, "Milton's Hexameter Patterns—Vergilian or Ovidian?" Vol. 93 No. 1 *American Journal of Philology* (1972) at 52-60.

1.22   The term *Tomitano* ("of Tomis") refers to the modern Constanta in Romania, where Ovid in his exile wrote many great works and died. Almost surely for humorous effect, Milton overdramatically associates his own brief absence from college with Ovid's exile from Rome. See Condee "Ovid's Exile and Milton's Rustification" Volume 37 *Philological Quarterly* (1958) at 498-502.

1.23   Homer was thought to have been born in Smyrna in Ionia.

1.27   Scholars long thought that Milton's knowledge of theatre was second-hand, but during Milton's adolescence his father was one of four trustees of the famed Blackfriars Theatre and it is likely that Milton was highly familiar with the drama of his time. See generally Burbery at 57-76. Burbery at 62 notes that *sinuosi pompa theatri* appears to be a conflation of Ovid *Amores* 1.89 (*curvis theatris*) and Propertius 4.1.15 (*sinuosa cavo pendebant vela theatro*), but may stretch his thoughtful thesis too far by arguing that *sinuosi* should be translated as "curved" because it is a reference to the distinctive shape of the Blackfriars building. Others have translated it as "winding" "hollow" or "curved," but I think the Propertius allusion with its use of *cavo* (probably "open area") suggests Milton is using *sinuosi...theatri* to refer to an Elizabethan theatre with a semicircular stage that is only partially roofed. The echo of Ovid here suggests an undercurrent of sexual longing; Ovid describes the *curvis...theatris* as prime places to pick up women.

For a list of Milton's later mentions of the theater, see MacKellar at 193.

1.29   Bush suggests that the phrase *prodigus haeres* ("a long-lost heir") may be drawn from Mantuan. See Bush, Shaw &

Giamatti at 51. There has been unproductive academic speculation as to which plays Milton might have been referring to here and in the following seventeen lines.

1.32   Part of the wit of this line stems from the near-certainty that the *barbara verba* ("foreign words") are Latin.

1.34   The phrase *nasum fallit* ("sneaks beneath the nose") has occasionally distressed scholars. See e.g. Kerrigan at 390 ("We doubt if *nasum fallit* be correct either in Latin or logic."). I found no classical precedent and took it as a tongue-in-cheek rendering of a trope that persists in recent colloquial English.

The 1673 edition does not capitalize *Patris*.

1.36   This line's *Quid sit amor nescit* ("knows nothing of love"—literally "does not know what love would be") echoes Ovid *Metamorphoses* 4.330 (*Nescia quid sit amor*). This couplet closes with the use of the classical rhetorical devices of chiasmus and paradox, which perhaps is an example of sophomoric showing off.

l. 39   The 1645 edition has a comma instead of a semicolon at the end of the line.

1.39-40   These lines are perhaps best read as a brief interjection interrupting the litany. Cf. n.36.

l.42   The 1645 edition has a comma, not a semicolon, after *cadit*.

1.43   In mythology the River Styx flowed between Earth and Hades. The image was so powerful for Milton he retained it in *Paradise Lost*. Cf. 1.239 ("Stygian flood").

The 1645 edition has no comma after *ultor*.

l.44   The 1645 edition has a comma instead of a semicolon after *movens*.

Fletcher notes a parallel to Ovid *Metamorphoses* 8.512 (*funereum torrem*).

1.45   Pelops was a prince sacrificed by his father, Tantalus, as a meal for the gods. By the time the gods discovered this ill-advised culinary choice, Pelops' shoulder had already been eaten. The gods brought Pelops back to life with a shoulder made of ivory and tortured Tantalus in Hades. The House of Pelops (Atreus, Thyestes, Agamemnon, Iphigenia, Electra, Orestes) was doomed. Cf. Milton *Il Penseroso* 99.

Ilus was the founder of Troy (hence "Ilium" as a name for the city). He lost his sight through an act of impiety but regained it by praying to Athena.

1.46   Creon, the brother-in-law of Oedipus, succeeded him as King of Thebes, hence the reference to incest.

1.48   Van De Walle at 27 notes that *tempora veris eunt* ("springtime... pass") is a conflation of two recurring Ovidian phrases. Revard (1997) at 15 notes that Renaissance love elegists invariably connected the sight of the beloved with the arrival of spring. Cf. 1.51-52.

1.49-50   These lines may be posturing that echoes Ovid's laments contrasting Tomis to the glories of Rome. See Condee, "Ovid's Exile and Milton's Rustification" Volume 37 *Philological Quarterly* (1958) at 498-502.

1.51   The phrase *spirantia...flammas* ("diffusing...beams") is Virgilian. Cf. *Georgica* 3.34 (*spirantia...flammas*). Cf. Ovid *Ars Amatoria* 1.59.

1.52   For *choros* as "bands" (in line 51 of the translation), cf. *Paradise Lost* 11.208 ("Heav'nly bands").

Fletcher notes the parallel to Pseudo-Seneca *Hercules Oetaeus* 593 (*virgineos...choros*).

1.57   For Pelops, see n.1.45 *supra*.

1.58   With the new technology of the telescope, Galileo proved that the Milky Way consisted of stars in 1610, about sixteen years before the composition of this elegy. See Wood "Milton and Galileo" Vol. 35 No. 1 *Milton Quarterly* (2001) at 50-52. Revard (1997) at 16 suggests that this line refers to the girls' white breasts, but I think that reading reflects a mistranslation of *quaeque* ("each"), which I believe refers back to *collaque* ("And necks") of the previous line.

1.60   There is a period, not a comma, after *Amor* in the 1645 edition, but I have treated it as a typographical error in my translation.

Fletcher notes the parallel to Seneca *Phaedra* 634 (*fallax Amor*).

1.61   The *hyacynthia* ("hyacinths") evokes the myth that the blood of a young male admired by Apollo stained the flower. See e.g. Homer *Iliad* 2.595-600; Ovid *Metamorphoses* 10.162-219; cf. Milton *On the Death of a Fair Infant Dying of a Cough* 22-28.

1.62   For Adonis, cf. Ovid *Metamorphoses* 10.503-739.

1.63   The term *Heroides* ("heroines") echoes the work of Ovid by that name.

1.65   The adjective *Achaemeniae* ("Persian') referred to the Parthian empire, which largely overlaps with modern Iran. Masson at 301 and MacKellar at 197 suggest that Milton picked up this observation about high headwear from *Travels* by George Sandys (1572-1644).

1.66   Susa (modern Shush) was a Persian city, at times the capital.

Memnon was an Ethiopian king who came to the defense of Troy but was killed by Achilles. Memnon ruled Persia, including the spectacular city of Nineveh. Cf. Milton *Il Penseroso* 18-19. The likely influence of Sandys mentioned in the previous note tends to reinforce Bush's suggestion that *Memnoniamque* ("Memnon's"—literally "Memnonian") in this line may also have come from Sandys. See Bush, Shaw & Giamatti at 55. MacKellar at 197 argues (wrongly, I believe) that the choice of this word reflects confusion of Susa with Nineveh.

1.69-70 The phrase *Tarpeia Musa* ("The Tarpeian Muse") refers to Ovid. Prior to his exile Ovid lived near the Tarpeian Rock, a cliff used for executions. The *Pompeianas...columnas* ("Pompey's colonnade") was in the more fashionable Campus Martius,

Bookstores were typically sited around columns of buildings. Ovid felt that bookstores and theatres were prime places to pick up women. See Ovid *Ars Amatoria* 1.67, 3.387.

1.71   In the 1645 edition there is a comma, not a semicolon, after *Britannis*.

1.72   I have not avoided the patriotic *double entendre* of this line, and thus I have rendered *sequi* as "coming next." For Milton's prolific sexual punning in this time period, see Shawcross (1993) at 40-43.

1.73   Continuing the patriotic fervor of the previous line, Milton here invokes the myth, popularized by the usually fictional *Historia Regum Britanniae* of Geoffrey of Monmouth, that Brutus, a great-grandson of Aeneas (no relation to Caesar's famous betrayer), founded London.

1.74   Translation of this line presents several challenges. I have translated *caput* (literally "head") as "crown" to stress the sense of "top of the head." The adjective *turrigerum* ("towering") literally means "tower-bearing," but the "tower-bearing head" would capture little of the meaning or flavor of the original Latin.

1.76   For *pendulus orbis* ("the pendulous world"), cf. *Paradise Lost* 2.1052 ("This pendant world'), 4.100 ("The pendulous round Earth"). This recurring image of a suspended Earth requires a majestic perspective that captures the comparative smallness of mankind.

1.77   The phrase *caelo...sereno* ("in cloudless sky") was common in Virgil and elsewhere in classical poetry. See e.g. *Aeneid* 3.518, 5.870; *Georgics* 1.260, 1.487.

1.78   Endymion was a Greek shepherd and lover of Selene, the goddess of the moon. Milton's likely source is the *Argonautica* of Apollonius of Rhodes.

1.81   For *geminis...columbis* ("by twin doves"), cf. Virgil *Aeneid* 6.190 (*geminae...columbae*).

1.83   The ancient port of Cnidus, which had a famous temple of Venus, was in modern Turkey.

The Simois River runs through the Trojan plain; Simois was also the name of a minor river God who defended Troy. Cf. Homer *Iliad* 21.311-315.

1.84   Paphos was a port on the west side of Cyprus, an island sacred to Venus. Paphos was also the name of a resident of the town who was the son of Pygmalion. Cf. Ovid *Metamorphoses* 10.238-297. Some considered Paphos the birthplace of Venus.

1.85   The *pueri...caeca* ("the blind boy's") refers to Cupid. Milton would not have anticipated his future blindness at the time he wrote these elegies.

1.87-88   The herb moly protected Odysseus from the witch Circe. See Homer *Odyssey* 10.305.

1.89   For *iuncosas cami...paludes* ("the Cam's reed-choked bogs"), cf. n.1.11 *supra*. Cf. Milton *Comus* 636.

1.92   The phrase *alternos...modos* ("uneven meters") is a reference to elegiac couplets, which alternate hexameter and pentameter lines.

2 Title   A *praeconis* was a crier for academic ceremonies, often called a "beadle." This elegy was probably written in the fall of 1626 after the death of Cambridge University's beadle, Richard Ridding. For Milton's use of classical rhetorical techniques in this and the other "funeral elegies," see West

"The 'Consolatio' in Milton's Funeral Elegies" Volume 34 No. 3 *Huntington Library Quarterly* (1971) at 233-245. The University still owns four silver-gilt maces presented by the Duke of Buckingham in 1626, the year Milton wrote this elegy. See MacKellar at 200.

2.1 The term *baculo* ("mace") refers to a staff used in academic ceremonies.

For a discussion of the relation of this poem as well as Elegies III and IV to Renaissance funeral elegy, see Revard (1997) at 44-51.

2.2 The term *Palladium* ("Athena's") refers to Pallas Athena, the goddess of learning. By calling his fellow students *gregem* ("flock"), Milton may be calling his fellow students a congregation or implying that they are reminiscent of sheep (or both).

2.5-6 These lines refer to the myth of Jove, the most powerful of the gods, who disguised himself as a swan in order to rape Leda. Ovid compares his own white hair to Leda's white feathers at *Tristia* 4.8.1-2.

2.7-8 These lines refer to the potion from Thessaly (otherwise known as "Haemonia") that Medea used to revive Jason's father. Cf. Ovid *Metamorphoses* 7.251-293: *Comus* 638.

2.9-10 These lines refer to Asclepius (or Aesculapius), the son of Coronis, for bringing Hipploytus back to life. Cf. Ovid *Metamorphoses* 7.263-293. Revard (1997) at 48-49 argues this reference reflects Milton's interest in Pindar.

For the River Styx and its Stygian waves, see n.1.43 *supra*.

2.12   The phrase *tuo...Phoebo* ("your Phoebus") is probably a sly reference to the head of the university or another administrator. Bush is overly sure it is a reference to the Vice-Chancellor of the University. See Bush, Shaw & Giamatti at 62. There is no comma after *tuo* in the 1645 edition even though the context clearly requires one.

2.13   The name *Cyllenius* refers to Hermes, a flying messenger for other gods, by referring to his place of birth on Mount Cyllenus. MacKellar could not find a reference for Hermes being sent to the palace of Priam, but notes a meeting outside the palace on the plains of Troy at Homer *Iliad* 24.334-357.

2.15-16   For Hermes' trip to Troy and subsequent actions involving Achilles and Atrides, see n. 2.13 *supra* and Homer *Iliad* 23.336-437. Eurybatus, like Hermes and the subject of this poem, was a herald; Agamemnon sent him to Troy during the Trojan War. *Id.* at 23.318-344.

2.17   The noun *Averni* ("Avernus"—from the Greek for "without birds" due to sulfuric fumes) is a lake in a volcanic crater in Southern Italy that was believed to be the entrance to Hades. Cf. Virgil *Aeneid* 6.106-107. In this line it is a metonym for Pluto, the god of the underworld; his "companion" would be Proserpine.

2.19   For divergent views on the source of *pondus inutile terrae* ("Earth's useless burdens"), see Bush, Shaw & Giamatti at 63.

          The 1645 edition has a comma instead of the clearly correct question mark of the 1673 edition.

3 Title	The famed preacher Lancelot Andrewes died on September 25, 1626, and Milton probably wrote this elegy shortly thereafter. In Chapter III of his 1641 tract *The Reason of Church Government*, Milton attacked Andrewes' views; this change of heart may be one of the main reasons for Milton's distancing of himself from these elegies in the untitled epigram added to *Elegiarum Liber*. But see Revard (1997) at 49 (suggesting Milton might have separated the man and his role).
3.2	Milton's use of the term *tristia* ("griefs") again associates his misery with Ovid's exile poems of the same title.
3.3-4	Libitina was the goddess of corpses, and here Milton is using her as a symbol for the plague that ravaged London throughout the previous year. See generally Hackenbracht at 403-438.
3.6	MacKellar at 202 notes the parallel to Ovid *Heroides* 2.120 (*sepuchrali…face*).
3.9	These lines probably refer to Count Ernest von Mansfeld and Duke Christian of Brunswick-Wolfenbuttel **[umlaut over u]**, who were Protestant supporters of the Palatine Elector during the Thirty Years War. But see Bush, Shaw & Giamatti at 65-67.
3.12	There is scholarly debate, but no consensus, as to who the *amissos…ducos* ("lost leaders") were who died fighting in the Low Countries.
3.13	There may be a semicolon rather than a comma at the end of this line, but since a comma is clearly correct I used the comma.

3.14   Translators tend to translate *gloria* as "glory," but I chose a word more often used to describe an honored pillar of a community.

3.16   The phrase *Tartareo...Iovi* ("Hell's Jove") is a reference to Pluto, the god of the underworld. Cf. Milton *Comus* 20 ("nether Jove").

For *mors fera* ("Fierce Death"), see Hackenbracht at 428-429. The 1645 edition does not have the 1673 edition's comma after *fera*.

3.20   The appellation *Cypridi* ("Venus") was a common one for Venus, who was associated with lushness and beauty of the island. Sometimes it was considered her birthplace.

The 1645 edition transposed a period and a question mark at the ends of 3.20 and 3.22.

3.22   See 3.20 *supra*.

Fletcher notes the parallel to Tibullus 1.1.28 (*praetereuntis aquae*).

3.23   The phrase *liquido caelo* ("through open sky") was probably Ovidian. Cf. *Metamorphoses* 1.23 (*liquidum caelum*).

3.25   Fletcher notes the parallel to Horace *Odes* 1.21.7-8 (*nigris... siluis*).

3.26   The elusive water god *Proteos* ("Proteus") herded Neptune's seals. In Book 4 of Homer's *Odyssey* Menelaus captures Proteus and forces him to disclose the way home. Cf. Milton *Paradise Lost* 3.604-606.

3.32	Born of a mortal and a god, Hesperus personified the evening star. The phrase *Roscidus...Hesperus* ("dewy Hesperus") is an Ovidian flourish. Cf. Ovid *Fasti* 2.314 (*Hesperos...roscidus*).
	Fletcher notes the parallels to Ovid *Tristia* 4.3.4, *Fasti* 1.314 (*occiduas...aquas*).
3.33	For *Tartessiaco* as "Atlantic," see Bush, Shaw & Giamatti at 72; MacKellar at 205.
3.35	The 1645 edition has either a period or comma, not a semicolon, at the end of the line.
3.36	The 1645 edition has a period, not a comma after *meos*. This line is one of the examples of an instance where the punctuation affects translation.
3.37	The 1645 edition has a comma, not a semicolon, after *agro*.
3.41	The phrase *Thaumantia proles* ("Iris"—literally "Thaumas' descendant") refers to the minor deity associated with the rainbow. Cf. Milton *Comus* 992-999.
3.43-44	The names *Zephyro* ("Zephyrus") and *Chloris* ("Chloris") refer to the god of the west wind and the goddess of flowers, respectively. Cf. Ovid *Fasti* 5.195-378. The name *Alcinoi* ("Alcinous") referred to a minor king mentioned in the tales of Jason and the Argonauts. Cf. *At a Vacation Exercise in the College* 49; *Paradise Lost* 5.341, 9.441. For his garden, cf. Homer *Odyssey* 7.112-132.
3.46	In classical poetry the Tagus was the obligatory river for golden sands. See e.g. Catullus 29.19; Ovid *Amores* 1.15.34;

Metamorphoses 2.251; Juvenal 3.55; Martial 1.49.15, 7.88.7; Silius *Punica* 16.450.

3.47   The appellation *Favoni* ("the West Wind") is another name for Zephyr. See n.3.44 *supra*.

3.49-50   For Lucifer's *domus* ("home"), cf. Ovid *Metamorphoses* 2.1-5.

For *nitido...in ore* ("on his shining face), cf. *Exodus* 34:29-35.

3.51-62   Milton mixes the past and present tenses in his narrative in a way consistent with classical, but not contemporary, narratives, so I have sometimes translated Latin verbs in the past tense into the present tense.

3.52   The precise meaning of *pellucentes* ("shining"—a rare and later version of the classical *perlucentes*)...*locos* ("points in space") is unclear.

3.56   In the early Christian era an *infula* ("miter") was worn on the head by priests; in Milton's era it typically referred to the ribbon on a bishop's mitre and here appears to used for the mitre itself..

3.60   For *triumphali...tuba* ("a triumphant trumpet"), see Hackenbracht at 428-430.

3.61   In the 1645 edition it is unclear whether the line ends with a semicolon or a comma, but context argues for a comma.

3.62   The phrase *placido...ore* ("a tranquil face") was common. See e.g. Virgil *Aeneid* 7.194, Ovid *Metamorphoses* 8.703, 11.282.

3.64   Cf. *Revelation* 14:13.

3.65	Cf. *Revelation* 14:2.
3.66	For *aurea...quies* as "golden slumber," cf. Milton *L'Allegro* 146 ("golden slumber"). Knight argues that this line is a conflation of Ovid *Amores* 1.5.26 and Tibullus 1.1.48. See "Juvenes ornatissimi: the student writing of George Herbert and John Milton" in Houghton & Mandwald at 62.
3.67	The appellation *Cephalia* ("Cephalus") refers to an early Greek hero kidnapped by Aurora, goddess of the dawn. Like many of the randy male deities, she got around. Cf. *L'Allegro* 19-24; n.5.49, n.7.37. n.7.39 *infra*. In the 1645 edition the lines ends with a comma, not a semicolon.
3.68	Scholars have puzzled over this line's echo of Ovid's wish for more daytime trysts with Corinna in *Amores* 1.5.26.
4.Title	Thomas Young was a Scottish clergyman who tutored the pre-teen Milton and later became his anonymous co-author of tracts under the name of SMECTYMNUUS . Milton defended his mentor and friend in his 1642 pamphlet *Apology for Smectymnuus*, despite some signs of philosophical tensions between the two stemming from Milton's support for divorce and Young's acceptance of emoluments from the government. Hamburg was a vulnerable stronghold of the Protestants during the Thirty Years' War.
4.1-2	These lines echo Ovid *Tristia* 3.7.1-2, and the practice of orally addressing a letter before sending it was popular among classical poets.

The 1645 edition has a comma, not a semicolon, at the end of line 2. I have translated the couplet as if there were a period in that location.

4.3   The phrase *Segnes…moras* ("dull delays") may echo Seneca *Medea* 1.0.54 (*segnes moras*) or Virgil *Georgics* 3.42-43.. Bush notes that the phrase *rumpe moras* ("End…delays") was common. Bush, Shaw & Giamatti at 81. Milton may have been hoping for speed because this elegy was sent with a letter in which Milton apologized for not writing for three years. Young's gift of a Hebrew Bible seems to have stirred Milton's epistolary skills. Campbell & Corns at 37.

4.4   The phrase *remoretur iter* ("let…slow your journey") echoes Ovid *Metamorphoses* 11.233 (*remoretur iter*).

4.5   For Aeolus, cf. Ovid *Metamorphoses* 24.224.

4.6   For *virides…Deos* ("young gods"), cf. Ovid *Tristia* 1.2.59 (*virides deos*). The adjective *virides* is often translated here and in Ovid with its primary meaning of "green," but here I think it means "young" (we still have a slang sense of that meaning in English) and incorporates the sense popularized in early Christian poetry that the power of the classical gods weakened over time. *Deos* is capitalized in the 1645 edition.

4.7   Doris was the wife of Nereus, a sea-god, and mother of the sea nymphs known as Nereids. Milton describes a similarly tranquil sea at *Lycidas* 96-99. Cf. Spenser *Faerie Queene* 4.11.48.

4.10 The *Colchis* here (literally "the Colchian") is Medea. The particular incident to which Milton is referring was probably inspired by Ovid *Heroides* 6.129-138.

For *ore* as "sight," see OLD 10.

The 1645 edition has a period at the end of this line.

4.11-12 For Triptolemus in his dragon-drawn chariot, cf. Ovid *Metamorphoses* 5.642-650. Eleusis (literally "the Eleusinian city") was the site of the Eleusinian mysteries; those who participated in its rites believed that initiation granted them an afterlife.

4.15-16 For sources for the Hama story, see Bush, Shaw & Giamatti at 82.

4.19 The 1645 edition appears to have a period or comma at the end of the line.

4.19-20 Revard (1997) at 158 notes that this phrase seems to echo either a reference by Aristophanes in Plato *Symposium* 189c-193e or Horace *Carmina* 1.3.8.

4.23 The *doctissime Graium* (literally "wisest of the Greeks") here is Socrates.

4.24 I have paraphrased this line to avoid obscurity and the metrical challenge of a very long and dense line. Literally, it is perhaps best rendered as "the son of Clinias (i.e. Alcibiades), who was the great-grandson of Telamon."

The 1645 edition has a period, not a semicolon, at the end of the line.

4.25 The appellation *Stagirites* (literally "the Stagirite") refers to Aristotle, who was the tutor of Alexander the Great.

4.26   This line describes the mythical parentage of Alexander the Great. Cf. *Paradise Lost* 9.508-509.

4.27   The son of Amyntor was Phoenix, who slept with his father's mistress to please his mother and unsuccessfully tried to mediate the breach between Achilles and Agamemnon during the Trojan War.

          For metrical reasons I have compressed *Myrmidonum regi* (literally "the King of the Myrmidons") to "the Ant-King." *Myrmidonum* comes from the Greek for "ant-people." Cf. Ovid *Metamorphoses* 7.474. I have also connected the two parallel phrases with an "and" to avoid the ambiguity of a more "literal" translation.

          Fletcher notes the parallel to Ovid *Metamorphoses* 2.676 (*Philyreius heros*).

4.28   *Philyreius* was a centaur commonly known as Chiron.

4.29   For a discussion of the proper definition and syntactical location of *Primus* ("first"), see Bush, Shaw & Giamatti at 84.

4.30   The phrase *bifidi...iugi* ("cleft mountain's") refers to double-peaked Mount Parnassus, a sacred place for Apollo and his poets in Aonia. Cf. *Paradise Lost* 1.14-15.

          The 1645 edition has a comma, not a semicolon, at the end of the line.

4.32   Clio was the Muse of history. The Castalian spring at the foot of Mount Parnassus was a familiar image; drinking from the spring was said to nourish one's poetic inspiration.

4.33   Aethon was a common name for a horse in classical poetry. See e.g. Ovid *Metamorphoses* 2.153; Homer *Iliad* 8.184; Virgil *Aeneid* 11.89.

4.34   The *veterum…volumina patrum* ("ancient Father's… volumes") refers to the Greek and Latin writings of early Christian authors. Chloris (aka Floris) was the goddess of flowers.

4.36   Auster was the south wind.

4.39   Eurus was the east wind.

The 1645 edition has a comma, not a semicolon, at the end of the line.

4.42   For *pignora* as "children" instead of "pledges" or "tokens," see OLD 4. The synonym "offspring" captures a little more of the sense of "products of a loving relationship."

4.44   The 1645 edition has a period, not a semicolon, at the end of the line.

4.45   Fletcher notes the parallel to Ovid *Fasti* 1.312 (*caelesti rore*).

4.49   MacKellar at 213 notes the close parallel to Ovid *Amores* 3.6.67 (*oculos in humum defixa modestos*).

4.50   For *ore* as "eloquence," see OLD 4b.

4.53   The 1645 edition has no punctuation at the end of the line.

4.55   In line 4.56 of the translation I have tried to imitate the playful *sera/vera* internal rhyme with stale/tales.

4.56-57	These lines are based on Ovid's embroidered retelling of Odysseus' return to Penelope in Book 23 of Homer's *Odyssey*. Cf. Ovid *Heroides* 1.1. 66.
4.58	In the 1645 edition there is a period, not a question mark, at the end of his line—a clear typographical error.
4.61	MacKellar at 213 notes that *da veniam fasso* ("give pardon to the pardon-seeker") was a very common Ovidian phrase.
4.65	The adjective *sarissiferi* ("spear-bearing") appears to have been coined by Milton. See Bush, Shaw & Giamatti at 88.
4.68	The 1645 edition capitalizes *Deos*.
4.69	The phrase *fuit impetus* ("he has been moved") is Ovidian.
4.71	For *Fama* ("Gossip"), cf. the allegory in Virgil *Aeneid* 4.173-195. See generally Bush, Shaw & Giamatti at 88.
4.74	Kerrigan, Rumrich & Fallon at 183 suggest these "Saxon lords" were Dukes Frederick, William and Bernard.
4.75	Enyo was the goddess of war. Cf. Homer *Iliad* 5.333, 592.
4.77	The 1645 edition has a comma, not a semicolon, at the end of the line.
	MacKellar notes that northern Thrace was believed to be a favored location of Mars.
4.78	The Odrysian steeds are probably taken from Homer *Odyssey* 8.361. These horses would have come from modern Thrace, the birthplace of Mars.

4.79	The *Diva* (in line 80 of the Latin) is Eirene, goddess of peace.
4.81-82	The words *virgo* ("girl") and *iusta* ("deserving") refer to Astraea, the goddess of justice. Cf. Ovid *Metamorphoses* 1.149-150.
4.82	Fletcher notes the parallel to Ovid *Metamorphoses* 4.735-736 (*superas domos*).
4.85	The 1645 edition has no punctuation at the end of the line.
4.87	The *saxis...albis* ("chalky rocks") are almost surely the white cliffs of Dover. Cf. OLD 2e
4.89	The phrases *exponere foetus* ("expose your newborns") refers to the classical practice of leaving deformed or otherwise unwanted babies exposed to the elements to die.
4.92	I have rendered *perspiciens* as "watchful" but it could also be translated as "foresighted."
4.97	The *vates...Thesbitidis* ("Tishbite prophet") is Elijah. Cf. 1 *Kings* 17.1.
4.100	Jezebel, the wife of King Ahab, threatened Elijah and caused him to flee to the desert. See 1 *Kings* 19:11-4.
4.101-102	For more on this description of Saint Paul, see *Acts* 16:22-35.
4.102	The 1645 edition has a period, not a semicolon, at the end of this line.
4.103	For more on the visit of Jesus to Gergessa, see *Matthew* 8:28-34.

4.105   Bush refers to this line as a "tissue of stock phrases." Bush, Shaw & Giamatti at 91.

4.111   In the 1645 edition there is a period, not a semicolon, at the end of the line. Either way the punctuation is puzzling.

4.113-114 For more on this battle, see 2 *Kings* 19:35-36.

4.115   The 1645 edition does not have a comma at the end of the line.

4.115-116 For more on these events, see 2 *Kings* 7:6-7; cf. Virgil *Aeneid* 8.588-594.

4.120   Despite the Christian nature of this poem, many translators literally render *lares* as "household gods" or something similar instead of treating it as a metonym for "hearth" or "home."

4.122   My end-rhyme here mimics the unusual end-rhyme in the original and the previous couplet.

5.Title   Revard (1997) at 17-18 argues that this elegy is less influenced by classical elegists than by Renaissance poets (such as Pontano, Sannazaro and Flaminio) who used elegiac couplets in their hymns to classical gods. These poets were in turn heavily influenced by Callimachus' "Hymn to Apollo."

5.2   For zephyrs, see n. 3.43-44.

5.5   Asking *fallor* (Am I fooled?) was a common Ovidian phrase.

5.6   The noun *ingenium* ("desire") could almost as easily be translated as either "talent" or "imagination."

5.6-7	The repetition of the phrase *munere veris adest* ("Spring's gift appears") across couplets in lines six and seven appears to be a playful twist on the technique of serpentine verse. Cf. 5.13-5.14.
5.7	The phrase *ab illo* ("because of it") is problematic here.
5.8	The 1645 edition does not have a question mark after *putet*.
5.9-10	Castalia is a spring on Mount Parnassus, a sacred place for poets often invoked seriously and humorously by poets. Pirene is a fountain that Pegasus, a winged horse, created with a hoof mark. Persius' *Prologue* to his *Satires* may be an inspiration here.
5.13-14	Daphne, a nymph and committed virgin who was the daughter of the river god Peneus. In most accounts Peneus transformed Daphne into a laurel tree to save her from Apollo's sexual aggression.
	The repetition of *Delius ipse venit* ("Apollo comes himself") at both ends of this couplet is an example of a Late Antique technique called "serpentine verse," which contemporary scholars tend to hold in low regard.
5.17	For associations between caves, poetry and prophecy in classical literature, see Bush, Shaw & Giamatti at 99.
5.18	The 1645 edition capitalizes *Deum* ("the gods' ").
5.22	This line may echo Lucan *Bellum civile* 7.551 (*haec rabies… iste furor*).

5.25-26 The Latin word for nightingale, *philomela*, probably reflected a continuation of thought from the reference to Daphne at 5.13-14. In most Latin accounts of the myth, Philomela was transformed into a nightingale after being raped and having her tongue ripped out. Cf. Ovid *Metamorphoses* 424-674; *Comus* 566; see also Revard (1997) at 20-21.

The tense of the vocative verb *adoperta* ("Begin") is frequently mistranslated.

5.29 Fletcher notes the parallel to Virgil *Aeneid* 12.840 (*celebrabit honores*).

5.30 For the 1673 text Milton appears to have edited the 1645 text from *perennis* ("yearly") to *quotannis* after his hated rival, Claude de Saumaise (also known as "Salmasius"), criticized his prosody for using *perennis* in this location in the line. Milton had criticized both Salmasius for his prose and Latin epigrams on a variety of grounds, including his lack of understanding of English words.

5.33 The 1645 edition does not have a comma at the end of the line.

Fletcher notes the parallels to Virgil *Aeneid* 4.123, 8.658, 10.161-162 (*nocte...opaca*).

5.36 The 1645 edition has a comma, not a semicolon, at the end of the line.

5.46 *Cynthia*, more commonly known as Artemis and Diana, was the goddess of nature and a protector of virginity. Cf. *On the Morning of Christ's Nativity* 101-108.

5.49   Aurora, the goddess of the dawn, was married to Tithonus, a Trojan prince. He was immortal but continued to age, and shriveled into little more than a voice. Marital relations presumably became impossible. See Revard (1997) at 21-22.

The 1645 edition has a comma, not a semicolon, at the end of the line.

5.51   Both for metrical reasons and for a connection to our contemporary cliché, I have translated *viridi...in herba* (literally "in green plants" as "in the weeds").

5.55-56   For Lucretian and Renaissance influences on romance between the sun and the earth, see Revard (1997) at 23-24.

5.57-58   Milton may be engaging in some complex but sophomoric wordplay here. The adjective *omniferos* ("all-bearing") appears to be a Miltonian invention based on a common suffix that may be having fun with bearing/baring. Cf. Milton *Metamorphoses* 1.672, 9.694 (*somniferis*). In other words, *omniferos...sinus* may be an interlingual pun with enough ambiguity to support denials of intent. The fact that the breasts are *luxuriosa* ("large") only fuels my suspicions.

5.62   Ops was another name for Cybele, a Phrygian fertility goddess who wore a high headdress. Her cult became very popular and was incorporated into the official Roman religion under Claudius. Mount Ida, located in modern Turkey, was sacred to Cybele.

5.66   For more on Proserpine, cf. Ovid *Metamorphoses* 5.385-408.

The 1645 edition capitalizes *Deo*.

For Zephyr, see 3.34-44 *supra*.

5.72   The 1645 edition has a comma, not a semicolon, at the end of the line.

5.76   The 1645 edition has a comma after *Munera*.

5.79   Fletcher notes the parallel to Ovid *Fasti* 3.415 (*cliuosum… Olympum*).

5.80   Flecther notes the parallel to Ovid *Metamorphoses* 4.92 (*praecipitatur aquis*).

5.82   The *caerula mater* ("sea-blue Mother") is Thetis, one of fifty sea nymphs and daughters of the sea god Nereus known as the Nereids. The epithet *caerula mater* ("sea-blue Mother") probably comes from Ovid *Metamorphoses* 13.288 (*caerula mater*).

5.83   Hesiod described Tethys as a Titan who was the daughter of Gaia and Uranus. Homer at *Iliad* 14.201 refers to her and Oceanus as the parents of the gods. Cf. *Comus* 870.

The 1645 edition has a comma, not a question mark, at the end of the line—a likely typographical error.

5.87   The 1645 edition has a comma, not a semicolon, after *herba*.

5.91-94   Semele was a mortal lover of Zeus and the mother of Dionysus. Cf. 3.253-315. As a result of jealously and deception by Hera, Semele was burned alive. Phaeton, son of Apollo and Clymene, was also burned alive when he tried to lead his father's sun-chariot. Cf. Ovid *Metamorphoses* 2.19-328.

5.101   For Diana, see n. 5.46 *supra*.

5.102   Vesta was the goddess of the hearth.

5.105-106 Hymen was the god of marriage. Cf. Ovid *Heroides* 12.143.

The 1645 edition does not italicize *Hymenaee* and *io Hymen*.

5.107   The 1645 edition has a comma, not a semicolon, at the end of the line.

5.108   Fletcher notes the parallel to Ovid *Fasti* 3.415 (*punicei... eroci*).

5.112   The name *Cytherea* was a common one for Venus; some myths placed Cythera as the island of her birth.

5.114   In pastoral poetry, Phyllis was a standard name for a shepherdess. See e.g. Virgil *Eclogae* 7.63, 10.37. 10.41.

5.118   For dolphins and music, see Pliny *Naturalis Historia* 9.8.24.

The 1645 edition capitalizes *Deos*.

5.120   Fletcher notes the parallel to Virgil *Aeneid* 1.430 (*florea rura*).

5.121   Milton adopts Virgilian rather than Ovidian mythology here. According to Virgil, Silvanus, god of the forest, accidentally killed a deer loved by Silvanus' love interest, a boy named Cyparissus, who died of grief and was then transformed into a cypress. See Virgil *Eclogae* 1.20; Servius *In Vergilii Aeneidos Commentarios* 3.680.1; but see Ovid *Metamorphoses* 10.106-142.

Fletcher notes the parallel to Virgil Aeneid 54.459 (*fronde reuinctum*).

5.125 Pan was the Greek god of shepherds and flocks; Maenalus was his sacred mountain in Arcadia.

5.126 For Cybele, see n.5.26 *supra*. Ceres was Cybele's daughter and the goddess of agriculture.

The 1645 edition does not have a semicolon at the end of this line.

5.127 Faunus was a Roman god of the woods and Oreads were mountain nymphs. He had goat-like features and the sex drive associated with goats.

5.128 Flecther notes the parallel of Ovid *Metamorphoses* 4.100 (*trepido pede*).

5.129 Webster at 69 notes that the phrase *male tecta* ("covered badly") echoes Maximianus 1.70 (*male tecta*) and this couplet somewhat parallels Maximianus 1.66-70. Due to the Pomponius Gauricus fraud of 1501, Milton probably thought he was echoing the elegies of Gallus, which are still largely lost.

5.136 Jove's *aspera tela* ("vicious weapons") are thunderbolts.

5.140 This line's *nostro…polo* ("our sky") may constitute some phallic wordplay around the alternate translation "pole."

6.Title Charles Diodati was Milton's closest friend.

6.3 Most commentators see *camoenam* ("Muse") as a synonym for *Musa* ("Muse"), Bush suggests that *camoenam* had a more limited "national connotation" and that Milton may be "modestly deprecating his own verses." Bush, Shaw & Giamatti at 115. The 1645 edition does not capitalize *camoenam*.

6.6 The 1645 edition has a period, not a comma, after *queas*. This punctuation may be superior to the 1673 edition and affects the translation of *Nam* in 6.7.

6.8 The pun on "feet" as body part/verse unit was familiar in classical and medieval Latin poetry. The alternating lengths of the lines in an elegiac couplet may cause it to "limp"; bad poetry also "limps." There is clearly wordplay going on in this line, perhaps with the impotency undercurrent suggested by "untouched" and "limp." The use of *integer* ("untouched" here but with a broad range of possible meanings) may echo Horace's famous *Ode* 1.22.1 (*integer vitae scelerisque*).

6.9 Some commentators, perhaps carried away by their classicism, explain *hilariemque Decembrimque* ("cheery Christmastime") as a reference to the raucous Roman holiday of Saturnalia instead of indigenous undergraduate raucousness prior to a holiday.

The 1645 edition does not have a comma at the end of the line.

6.15-6.16 Bacchus, the god of wine, wore ivy garlands. Cf. Ovid *Metamorphoses* 3.664-665

6.17 There was no fully satisfying translation of *Euoe* ("O yeah!"), the drunken cry of Bacchus' followers. Thyone (aka Semele) was the mother of Bacchus. The 1645 edition does not italicize *Euoe*.

6.19 The 1645 edition has a colon, not a semicolon, at the end of the line.

6.20 Ovid's work during his exile in Tomis generally did not attain the level of his earlier works. Ovid considered the Coralli who lived in Tomis barbaric and portrayed them as wearing fur. See Ovid *Epistulae ex Ponto* 4.8.83.

6.21 Lyaeus was another name for Bacchus.

6.22 The Muse of Teos was Anacreon, an outstanding poet of the sixth century BC who was famous for his drinking poems.

6.23 Boeotia was one of the oldest areas of Greece; Thebes was its largest city.

Pindar, a Boeotian, was one of the greatest Greek poets; he was renowned for his odes, which he composed to celebrate athletic victories.

6.24 The 1645 edition has a period, not a semicolon, at the end of the line.

6.25-26 The "dust" in this quotation from Pindar refers to an Olympic track.

6.27 *Iaccho* is yet another name for Bacchus; Milton uses it as a metonym for wine.

6.27-28 Horace's *Odes* included women named Glycera and Chloe.

6.31	Massic and Falernian were favorite wines of Romans that were frequently mentioned in poetry.
6.32-33	For Phoebus/Apollo, see n.1.14 *supra*. For Ceres, see n.5.26 *supra*. For Bacchus, see n.6.15-16 *supra*. With the three gods and the wine, Milton is poking fun at more than classical religion.
6.36	The 1645 edition capitalizes *Deos*.
6.37	Orpheus, the god of music, was from Thrace, an area that includes modern Greece, Bulgaria and Turkey.
6.43	Although there has been some confusion among scholars about the *ebur* ("ivory") here, it is a reference to the pick (or "plectrum") used to pluck a lyre.
6.44	Fletcher notes the parallel to Ovid *Metamorphoses* 8.582, 8.746 (*festas…choreas*).
6.46	The 1645 edition has a comma, not a semicolon, at the end of the line.
6.48	Thalia was the Muse of comic and bucolic poetry.
	Translators are all over the map on *lapsa…sinus* ("wrecked heart"). It is possible that it might be a sly reference to the tradition in Roman love poetry that a sunken chest is a product of exhausting sexual activity.
6.50	The noun *numeros* ("numbers") may be an interlingual pun on "numbers" as a term denoting both meters and crowds.

6.51   Erato was the Muse of lyric and love poetry. Liber was the god of fertility and often associated with Dionysus but without as much association with wine.

6.58   The *latrata fero...cane* ("fierce howling dog") was Cerberus, who guarded the entrance to Hades.

6.59   Pythagoras was a polymath whose lifestyle was satirized by Horace and others. He was an ascetic and a vegetarian who believed in reincarnation.

6.60   The adjective *innocuos* here means "harmless" in two senses—Pythagoras believed vegetarianism was a healthy *and* moral diet.

6.63   The comma after *vacans* in the 1645 edition was removed in the 1673 edition.

6.64   Fletcher notes the parallel to Ovid *Remedia Amoris* 6.64 (*rigidos mores*).

Commentators generally pass over the masturbatory image at the end of this line, but when they do note it they usually fail to recognize its jokiness. See e.g. Quint at 203-204.

6.65   The phrase *lustralibus undis* ("cleansing waters") is probably a Christian image. See Bush, Shaw & Giamatti at 122; but see MacKellar at 231.

6.66   The 1645 edition capitalizes *Deos*.

6.68   Tiresias was a seer in Homer's *Odyssey* who was transformed into a woman and then back to a man; Hera struck him blind for opining that women enjoy sex more than men. He/she figures prominently in the poetry of Dante, Tennyson, Eliot and many others.

Linus was a figure, sometimes described as a music teacher with pupils such as Orpheus and Heracles; his story varied greatly depending on the teller.

Ogygia was the island (never definitively identified) where the nymph Calypso diverted Odysseus for seven years. See Homer *Odyssey* 5.58-74: but see Mackellar at 231.

6.69   Calchas was the seer of the Greek army at Troy.

6.73   In Book 10 of *The Odyssey*, the goddess Circe lived on the island of Aeaea. She bore several of Odysseus' children and turned his crew into pigs. The magician Comus is the son of Circe and Bacchus in Milton's *Comus*.

6.74   This line refers to the Sirens, female creatures whose ethereal songs lured sailors to their deaths on rocks.

6.75-76 Cf. Homer *Odyssey* 11.22-50.

6.81-90 These lines allude to Milton's 1629 ode *On the Morning of Christ's Nativity*.

6.85   The postclassical compound adjective *stelliparumque* ("star-spawning") spurred criticism from Milton's enemy Salmasius.

6.86   The 1645 edition capitalizes *Deos*.

6.89   The term *pressa* ("sober") has plagued translators. It could be either a participle or an adjective, and either choice has a range of meanings that alters the sense of the couplet.

	The 1645 edition has a comma, not a semicolon, at the end of the line.
7.1	The appellation *Amathusia* was another name for Venus because of her temple at Amathus.
7.2	Venus had a shrine at Paphos on Cyprus. Cf. Ovid *Amores* 2.17.4; n.1.84 *supra*.
7.5	The 1645 edition has a comma, not a semicolon, at the end of the line.
7.6	The 1645 edition has a period, not a semicolon, at the end of the line.
7.5-8	Intertwined tropes of war and love were common in love elegy. See e.g. Ovid *Amores* 1.1-16.
7.11	The appellation *Cyprius* for Cupid was rare, and recent for Milton.
7.12	The 1645 edition does not have a comma after *Promptior*.
7.13-14	For connections between this elegy and the tradition of "May elegies," see Revard (1997) at 27-28. This couplet would have immediately set off very festive, and perhaps erotic, associations for a reader in Milton's time. Although Herrick was a little older than Milton, his famous "Corinna going a-Maying" (which also includes a sleepy male not initially rising to the opportunities of May) postdated this elegy.
7.17	The 1645 edition has a comma, not a semicolon, at the end of the line.

7.18 The 1645 edition has a colon, not a semicolon, at the end of the line.

7.20 The 1645 edition has a comma after *puero*.

7.21 The *iuvenis Sigeius* ("Ganymede"—literally "the Sigean youth") was a young boy who was the object of Jove's sexual attentions and became his cupbearer. Cf. Ovid *Metamorphoses* 10.155-161.

7.22 There has been some scholarly debate about a printing error that suggests for some that *aethereo* ("heavenly") should be substituted for *aeterno* ("eternal").

7.24 Hylas was a boy who was the object of Heracles' sexual attentions. Adoring water-nymphs drew him into a spring, where he drowned. Cf. Apollonius *Argonautika* Book I.

7.27 The 1645 edition has a comma, not a semicolon, at the end of the line.

7.31 For Cupid's arrow of love shot at Apollo and his arrow of indifference shot at Daphne, see Ovid *Metamorphoses* 1.452-567.

7.35-36 The skill of Parthian (more-or-less modern Persian) horsemen was legendary.

7.37-38 The *Cydoniusque...venator* ("Cephalus"—literally "the Cydonian hunter") was an Aeolian prince kidnapped by Aurora, goddess of the dawn. He fathered a child by her but returned to his wife Procris, albeit uneasily. Cf. Ovid *Metamorphoses* 7.835-862; *Ars amatoria* 3.687-746.

7.39 Orion was created from the urine of three gods. Cf. Ovid *Fasti* 5.495. He was sexually pursued by Aurora, the goddess of the dawn, and he sexually pursued the Pleiades, the seven daughters of the Titan Atlas.

7.40 The *comes* ("friend") in this line probably refers back to Hylas in 7.23-24, although the scholarship on this point is all over the map. Cf. Ovid *Heroides* 9.47-100.

7.46 The *Phoebaeus...anguis* ("snake of Phoebus') was Ascelpius, the god of healing. Cf. Ovid *Metamorphoses* 626-744; n.2.9-10 *supra*.

7.47 For *aurato...sagittam* ("an arrow tipped with gold"), cf. Ovid *Metamorphoses* 1.468-471.

7.51 The 1645 edition does not have a comma at the end of the line.

7.51-7.52 Milton may be describing May Day processions.

7.55 Fletcher notes the parallel to Virgil *Georgics* 4.98 (*fulgore coruscant*).

7.56 For *Fallor* see note 5.5 *supra*.

7.58 The 1645 edition has a comma after *iuvenilis*.

7.61 The 1645 edition has a comma, not a semicolon, at the end of the line.

7.64 The *regina Deum* ("The queen of gods") is Juno, the sister and wife of Jupiter.

7.70	The 1645 edition has a colon, not a semicolon, at the end of the line.
7.73	The 1645 edition has a comma, not a semicolon, at the end of the line.
7.79	The 1645 edition has a comma, not a semicolon, after *Findor*.
7.81-82	This couplet, beginning with *amissum...coelum* ("he squandered Heaven") perhaps foreshadows *Paradise Lost*. Vulcan (literally "Juno's son"), the god of fire, was thrown from Olympus by Jove and landed on the island of Lemnos. Cf. Homer *Iliad* 1.590-593; cf. *Paradise Lost* 1.739-747.
7.83-84	Amphiaraus, one of the Seven Against Thebes, dropped down to Hades as he rode into a hole in the ground blown open by a bolt of lightning thrown by Jove.
7.85	The 1645 edition has *victus, amores* instead of *victus? Amores*.
7.88	The 1645 edition has a semicolon, not an exclamation point, at the end of the line.
7.90	The verb *surdeat* ("be deaf") was rare and recent for Milton. For a superb discussion of this verb, see generally Dillon; see also Le Comte at 123-124, Wordsworth at 48.
7.91	The 1645 edition has a comma, not a semicolon, at the end of the line.
7.92	For *ponar* as "I'll be declared," see OLD 18.
7.93	The 1645 edition has a comma, not a semicolon, at the end of the line.

7.97   Fletcher at 344 notes the parallel to Lucretius 6.752 (*fumant altaria donis*).

7.99   The 1645 edition has a comma, not a semicolon, after *furores*.

7.102   The phrase *amaturos…duos* ("a pair in love") is closer literally to "two who will love."

Untitled Postscript (Haec ego mente…)

1   Fletcher notes the parallel to Virgil *Aeneid* 2.54, *Eclogues* 1.16 (*mens…laeua*).

2   The use of the plural with *vana trophaea* ("pointless trophies") supports the view that this poem renounces many aspects of the seven elegies. But see Fallon at 77-78 (arguing it rejects only Elegy 7). Some translators soften *nequitiae* ("vileness"), but I judge the term to be a truly harsh self-assessment by a middle-aged man who regrets the views of his youth. But see Revard (1997) at 192 ("*Nequitiae* is possibly an echo of Ovid's disclaimer of his verse as trifles (*Amores* 2.2)"). Of course, lines 7-8 raise the question of whether this apology is entirely sincere and whether Milton regretted in line 8 that his "heart has stiffened."

5   The *umbrosia Academia* ("shaded school") is the school of Platonism, not Cambridge, as the next lines clarify. Cf. *Paradise Regained* 4.272-280.

6   For *iugum* ("the yoke"), cf. Milton *Paradise Lost* 2.256-257 ("Hard liberty before the easy yoke/Of servile pomp").

10   For Venus and Diomedes, cf. Ovid *Metamorphoses* 14.477-478.

On the Gunpowder Plot

2   Guy Fawkes was a conspirator in the 1605 Gunpowder Plot, a failed attempt to blow up Parliament and restore Catholicism as England's state religion.

3   For *Fallor?* ("Am I deceived?"), see n.5.5 *supra*.

7-8   These lines refer to Elijah. Cf. 2 *Kings* 2:7.

On the Same Subject I (Roman numerals added to this epigram and the next two for ease of citation)

1   King James died in 1625; Milton wrote this epigram and the following two shortly after James' death. Revard (1997) notes at 86 that these poems reflect anxiety that James' successor might not live up to his predecessor's ideals.

          The term *Belua* ("Beast") was a Protestant invective based on *Revelation* 13:1.

2   Rome, the site of the Vatican, is famous for its seven hills.

On the Same Subject II

1   King James condemned "Purgatorie and all the trash depending thereupon" in his *Premonition*.

On the Same Subject III

2   The "Taenarian harbor" was a gateway to Hades located on the central peninsula of the central Peloponnesus and its terminal cape. James was baptized a Catholic but raised a Protestant, so many Catholics consider him damned.

4   In the 1645 edition *Deos* is capitalized.

On the Inventor of Gunpowder

1   The term *Iaptionidem* ("the son of Iapetus") refers to Prometheus, who stole fire from Heaven and was tortured forever as punishment. Cf. *In obitum Procancellarii medici* 3 (*Iapeti...nepotes*). Prometheus was the son of Iapetus, a Titan often thought of as the god of mortality.

4   The phrase *lurida...arma* ("ghastly weapons") in line 3 of the original text may echo the unusual *lurida...tela* of Ovid *Tristia* 5.312.

To Leonora Singing in Rome

           Leonora Baroni (1611-1670) was a famous Italian singer and musician. Milton saw her perform in Rome during 1638-1639.

5   The phrase *mens tertia* ("a third mind") is a reference to the Neoplatonic concept of an elevated state of mind that can detect the most spiritual sounds. See McColley at 127-148; cf. Plato *Symposium* 2.4. Kerrigan, Rumrich & Fallon at 200 wrongly suggest that it is a reference to the third person of the Trinity, an interpretation I rule out both due to the introductory clause and, to a lesser extent, the bleakness of the *vacui...caeli* ("empty sky").

8   For metrical criticism, see MacKellar at 246.

On the Same Subject I (Roman numerals added to this epigram and the following one for ease of citation)

1	The wordplay of this line is impossible to capture. The *Torquato* is the famed Italian poet Torquato Tasso (1544-1595). *Torquato* also suggests the Latin verb *torque* (both "torture" and "twist"), arguably a metaphorical bridge to the subjects of lines 2-4. Cf. *Paradise Lost* 2.63-2.64 ("Turning our tortures into horrid arms/Against the Torturer.").

	In the 1645 edition *Poetam* is capitalized.

6	Leonora Baroni's mother, Adriana Basile, was also an accomplished musician.

7.	The Theban king Pentheus was a critic of the Dionysian rites, for which Dionysius drove him mad. Pentheus was dismembered by angry female Dionysians, including his mother.

On the Same Subject II

2	Parthenope was one of the Sirens; she drowned herself when Odysseus escaped and was buried in Naples. Cf. Ovid *Metamorphoses* 14.101. Leonora Baroni was also from Naples.

	Achelous was a river god. Cf. Ovid *Metamorphoses* 8.547-611, 9.1-97; Milton *Comus* 878-879.

8	In the 1645 edition *Deos* is capitalized.

Selected Sources

Boehrer, B. "The Rejection of Pastoral in Milton's 'Elegia Prima' " Vol. 99 *Modern Philology* (2001) at 181-200.

Brown, C. "John Milton and Charles Diodati: Reading the Textual Exchanges of Friends" Vol. 45 No. 2 *Milton Quarterly* (2011) at 73-94.

Burbery, T. "John Milton, Blackfriars Spectator? 'Elegia Prima' and Ben Jonson's The Staple of News" Vol. 10 *The Ben Jonson Journal* (2003) at 57-76.

Bush, D., Shaw, J & Giamatti, A. *A Variorum Commentary on the Poems of John Milton*. New York: Columbia University Press (1970).

Byard, M. "Adventurous Song: Milton and the Music of Rome" in DeCesare, M. (ed.) *Milton in Italy: Contexts, Images, Contradictions*. Binghamton: Medieval and Renaissance Texts and Studies 24 (1991) at 305-328.

Campbell, G. & Corns, T. *John Milton: Life, Work and Thought*. Oxford: Oxford University Press (2008).

Condee, R. "Ovid's Exile and Milton's Rustification" Vol. 37 *Philological Quarterly* (1958) at 498-502.

Dillon, J.: "*Surdeo*, Saumaise, and the Lexica" Vol. 27 *Humanistica Lovaniensa* (1978) at 238-252.

Duckworth, G. "Milton's Hexameter Patterns—Vergilian or Ovidian?" Vol. 93 No. 1 (1972) at 52-60.

DuRocher, R. *Milton and Ovid*. Ithaca: Cornell University Press (1985).

Fallon, S. *Milton's Peculiar Grace: Self-Representation and Authority*. Ithaca: Cornell University Press (2007).

Fletcher, G. "Milton's Latin Poems" Vol. 37 No. 4 *Modern Philology* (May 1940) at 343-350.

Glare, P. (ed.) *Oxford Latin Dictionary*. Oxford: Oxford University Press (2006). (abbreviated in notes as OLD)

Godolphin, F. "Notes on the Technique of Milton's Latin Elegies" Vol. 37 No. 4 *Modern Philology* (May 1940) at 351-356.

Haan, E. *John Milton's Latin Poetry: Some Neo-Latin and Vernacular Contexts*. Belfast: Queen's University of Belfast (1987).

Haan, E. *From Academia to Amicitia: Milton's Latin Writings and the Italian Academics*. Philadelphia: American Philological Society (1998).

Hackenbracht, R. "The Plague of 1625-1626, Apocalyptic Anticipation, and Milton's Elegy III" Vol. 108 No. 3 *Studies in Philology* (2011) at 403-438.

Hale, J. "The Punctuation of Milton's Latin Verse: Some Prolegomena" Vol. 23 No. 1 *Milton Studies* (March 1989) at 7-19.

Hale, J. *Latin Writings: a selection*. Assen: Bibliotheca Latinitatis Novae (1998).

Houghton, L. & Mandwald, G. (eds.) *Neo-Latin Poetry in the British Isles*. Bristol: Bristol Classical Press (2012).

Howatson, M. *The Oxford Companion to Classical Literature*. Oxford: Oxford University Press (2005).

Keightly, T. *The Poems of John Milton, with Notes* (Volume II) London: Chapman & Hall (1859).

Kerrigan, W., Rumrich, J. & Fallon, S. *The Complete Poetry and Essential Prose of John Milton*. New York: Random House (2007).

Kilgour, M. *Milton and the Metamorphoses of Ovid*. Oxford: Oxford University Press (2012).

Le Comte, M. *Milton Re-viewed*. Oxford; Routledge (1991).

MacKellar, W. *The Latin Poems of John Milton*. New Haven: Yale University Press (1930).

McColley, D. "Tongues of Men and Angels: *Ad Leonoram Romae Canentem*" Vol. 19 *Milton Studies* (1984) at 127-148.

Quint, D. "Expectation and Prematurity in Milton's Nativity Ode," Vol. 97 No.2 *Modern Philology* (1999) at 195-219.

Revard, S. *Milton and the Tangles of Neaera's Hair: The Making of the 1645 Poems*. Columbia: University of Missouri Press (1997).

Revard, S. *Complete Shorter Poems*. Malden: Wiley-Blackwell (2009).

Shawcross, J. "Form and Content in Milton's Latin Elegies" Vol. 33 *Huntington Library Quarterly* (1971) at 331-350.

Shawcross, J. *John Milton: the Self and the World.* Lexington: University Press of Kentucky (1993).

Tylawski, E. & Weiss, C. (eds.) *Essays in Honor of Gordon Williams: Twenty-Five Years at Yale.* New Haven: Henry R. Schwab (2001).

Van De Walle, K. "The Latin Development of John Milton's Poetical Voice in the 1645 *Poems*". M.A. thesis, Ghent University (2010).

Webster, R. *The Elegies of Maximianus.* Princeton: Princeton University Press (1900).

West, M. "The 'Consolatio' in Milton's Funeral Elegies" Vol. 34 *Huntington Library Quarterly* (1971) at 233-249.

Wood, D. "Milton and Galileo", Volume 35 No. 1 *Milton Quarterly* (2001) at 50-52.

Wordsworth, C. "On Some Faults in Milton's Latin Poetry" *Classical Review* (April 1887) Vol. 1 No 2/3 at 46-48.

Throughout the notes I have used the abbreviation "OLD" as a reference to: Glare, P. (ed.). *Oxford Latin Dictionary.* Oxford: Oxford University Press (1996).

Made in the USA
Middletown, DE
10 August 2019